The Terrible Speller

The
Terrible
Speller

A Quick and Easy Guide to
Enhancing Your Spelling Ability

William Proctor

QUILL
WILLIAM MORROW
NEW YORK

Library of Congress Cataloging-in-Publication Data

Proctor, William.
    The terrible speller / by William Proctor.
        p.   cm.
    ISBN 0-688-14229-X
    1. English Language—Orthography and spelling.   I. Title.
PE1145.2.P76   1993
428.1—dc20   93-21946
                                                                          CIP

Printed in the United States of America

First Quill Edition

1 2 3 4 5 6 7 8 9 10

BOOK DESIGN BY ANN GOLD

CONTENTS

1
Confessions of a Terrible Speller

After settling down in a taxi that was speeding from La Guardia Airport to my home in Manhattan, I was threatened by the driver. No, this is not one of your classic rip-off-the-customer stories that are rife in New York City. This time, the threat was to my pride.

"My last two fares, I couldn't believe," he said in a foreign accent I couldn't quite identify. "Most people in this country can't spell. They are supposed to be educated, and they can't even spell."

"What do you mean?" I said.

"I mean, I take English classes, to improve my speaking and writing, so I won't have to drive a cab all my life. And here was this well-dressed woman, obviously worth a lot of money. I asked her how to spell a common word, and she couldn't. It was the same with a man I picked up, an executive. He couldn't spell the word either."

Why did I have such a strong feeling I was being set up? Anyhow, I bit: "What was the word?"

" 'Sapphire,' " he said. "They couldn't even spell 'sapphire.' "

Then he stopped and waited. He didn't actually ask me to spell the word, but the challenge had been made. If I ignored him—or worse, if I spelled the word incorrectly—I risked humiliation *and* being added to his list of stupid American citizens who couldn't spell their way out of a paper bag!

So I gave it my best shot. I knew there was no *f* in the word. My problem was the *p*'s. Was there one or two? Following an old rule that had often worked for me in the past, I pronounced the word, pictured it in my mind's eye on an imaginary sheet of paper, and then went with my *first* impression (if you think about a tough word too much, you're almost certain to misspell it!).

"S-A-P-P-H-I-R-E."

"Yes, well, you obviously know, but they didn't," he said with what I was sure was a disappointed edge to his voice. "But I'm amazed at how many don't spell well."

I was so relieved I had passed the test that I hardly heard the man relate how one of his victims had used an *f* and the other had left out not only one *p* but the *e*.

An inability to spell can pose a serious threat to one's self-confidence. I know of at least one instance where a grown man cried at a meeting when a report he had written was criticized for poor spelling. It's little wonder that spelling often becomes an element in a person's most fundamental feelings of adequacy, because spelling is a bedrock language ability that supports all other communications skills. There are, of course, many excellent writers and powerful speakers who are poor spellers. Still, it's more likely that you'll write and speak with your *maxi-*

mum effectiveness if you're a reasonably competent speller.

Upwardly mobile managers, entrepreneurs, and professional types who spell well will often make an excellent impression in their written communications—even if clients, bosses, and other important colleagues don't know exactly why. You may hear a supervisor say of a good speller, "She writes a good letter."

Good spellers are also more likely to be adept at proper pronunciation—which is a key element in persuasive speaking. Many times, I've heard otherwise well-educated people say "grie*vi*ous" when they mean "grievous," or "ek cetera" when they mean "et cetera." The reason they make these mistakes is that they don't know how to spell the words!

Again, it usually won't register with listeners *why* a speaker is impressive or not so impressive. You'll probably never hear the one offering the praise suggest that the good performance can be traced to the person's spelling ability. Spelling is a skill that few notice—unless you make a mistake!

Yet when you *do* slip, you can expect a swift response, either to your face or behind your back. You can assume that someone somewhere is saying, "That shocks me, that he made a mistake like that." Or, "That guy just can't spell!" Or, "That woman must have missed sixth-grade English!"

Even if you would place yourself at the bottom of some sixth-grade English class right now, there's still hope. Anyone's spelling can be improved by some well-honed tricks. I know I don't have the greatest memory in the world, and so for most of my life, to pass muster as an adequate speller, I've had to rely mainly on the use of word associations, rhymes, or other mnemonic devices.

For years, I couldn't remember how to spell "weird." I'd first write "wierd," but then I'd decide that didn't look quite right. Next, I'd try the correct spelling, "weird." Somehow, though, *that* didn't look right either. (Tough words *never* seem to look quite right, do they?) In the end, I'd resort to the dictionary, but with a feeling of defeat, since I knew I wouldn't always have a library reference at hand.

How did I finally master "weird"? I devised a variation on an old spelling rhyme: "*i* before *e* except after *c*— and except in 'weird.' " Now, whenever I mutter that little line under my breath, I *always* know how to spell "weird"!

But don't get me wrong. To become a good speller, you don't have to fill your head full of hundreds of elementary-school ditties or rules. It's just a matter of learning a simple system that will allow you to be right most of the time.

My purpose in this book is to provide you with such a system. The relatively simple approach advocated in these pages may not be enough to make you into a National Spelling Bee champion, but it should certainly be sufficient to qualify you for an A in any employer's or colleague's grade book.

A Simple Strategy to Improve Your Spelling

In subsequent discussions, we'll be considering the correct spelling of many specific words, including the Toughest 228, which will be the subject of the next chapter. The important thing, though, is not just to memorize the spelling of certain important words. Rather, your goal should be to develop a *system* that will help you remember those words *and* increase your chances of spelling correctly many other words that you've never encountered in any special listing.

The following fundamental guidelines underlie the spelling strategy that will be detailed in this book:

1. Pronounce every word clearly before you try to spell it.

It's amazing the number of words that are misspelled because the writer misses a syllable or sound. For example, in one recent book I wrote I used the word for eye doctor, "ophthalmologist," a number of times. Yet to my embarrassment, I consistently misspelled it—primarily because I didn't pronounce the word properly.

I got the *ph* right (that is, I didn't use an *f*), but in my mind, I mispronounced the word: "oph-tha-mol-o-gist." In other words, I omitted the *l* sound in the second syllable, and as a result, I left that *l* out when I was writing.

The lesson: Pronounce the word correctly, and you'll greatly increase the odds that you'll spell correctly.

2. Use memory devices.

Employ whatever effective trick you can devise that will help you remember the spelling of a word. It doesn't matter how silly the memory device (or *mnemonic*) is; after all, you don't have to tell anyone your spelling secrets.

Take this word "mnemonic" that I've just used. That can be a hard one because the initial *m* is silent in the pronunciation. But if you know that the definition of the word "mnemonic" is "memory device," you're almost home. All you have to remember is that the word involves memory, and "memory" begins with an *m* too. (Note: The word is often used in the plural, "mnemonics," to mean a group of devices or comprehensive techniques to improve the memory.)

Sometimes the simplest, most effective memory trick is first to learn the correct pronunciation but then to *mis*-pronounce the word to highlight the correct spelling. I've found that technique useful with a word like "noticeable," which many people misspell by omitting the first *e*.

My own spelling memory periodically fails with "noticeable." One of the reasons for my problem is that I may begin to play mind games by comparing "noticeable" with similar-seeming words. For example, I know it's correct to write either "acknowledgement" or "acknowledgment" (either with the *e* or without). So why not two ways for "noticeable"? In the midst of such erroneous musings, I can usually jerk my mind back to the straight and narrow by this mispronunciation: "no-ti-*ceee*-a-ble." Turning a difficult silent *e* into a long *e* does wonders for spelling performance! (And as long as I learn the *correct* pronunciation first, I've never slipped into the mispronunciation when speaking.)

Such memory devices are one of the staples that are used throughout this book to improve your accuracy.

3. Learn some simple rules.
The English language is notorious for setting rules and then breaking them. Take plurals. You've heard that the

plural is usually formed by adding an *s*, as in "chairs." But what about the plural of "roach," which is "roaches"? Or worse, one of those highly irregular plurals like "children"?

Despite the inconsistencies and exceptions to many rules, there are some eternal laws of the spelling universe, such as the fact that *q* is always followed by a *u*.

(Actually, it could be argued that there are even some exceptions to this venerable precept, since a small number of words in large dictionaries begin with *qa,* including "qabbala," a variation on "cabala," the mystical system of Hebrew knowledge; and "qadi," a Muslim judge. But I would argue that these are not true English words; instead, they are Middle Eastern words that have been spelled using the English alphabet but not using ordinary English spelling conventions.)

Throughout this book, we'll be mentioning a number of rules like these, including both the ones with many exceptions and the few that are hard-and-fast law. If you're like me, you may have an aversion to learning and following a bunch of guidelines. But you'll find that there aren't as many as you might think, and they can be extremely helpful in increasing spelling accuracy.

4. Picture the word in your mind before you try to spell it.

Often, a little forethought or visualization will lead to tremendous decreases in spelling errors. A variation on this technique: Before you write the word for public consumption, jot down the two or three ways you think it *might* be spelled. This sort of trial run can often eliminate mistakes at the outset.

You might ask, why not just consult the dictionary rather than go to all this trouble? You're absolutely right that if you are uncertain about a word, you should take advantage of any opportunity to check the dictionary before you complete your draft. But sometimes it's not possible to use a dictionary.

In one informal business conference, an executive was asked to write out a short, two-sentence resolution that he had suggested the group adopt. The assignment, which had to be finished during a short break in the session, was to submit his draft to the chairman (the executive's boss) and a recording secretary before the meeting was reconvened.

This man began to scribble on a writing pad but quickly discovered that one of the words he had used in his proposal, "occasion," didn't look quite right—mainly because he had spelled it "occassion." He knew the problem lay in one of those sets of double letters. So he jotted the alternatives down on another sheet of paper and soon saw that the best candidate was "occasion," the correct spelling. Without actually seeing the word on paper, however, he would have misspelled it and perhaps lost face with his boss.

5. Go with the first impression.

I've already mentioned this principle in the description of my encounter with the New York City cab driver. The reason this guideline is so important is that spelling, perhaps of all the academic disciplines, is extremely vulnerable to "mind games." People can come up with the most logical reasons why they should write a word a certain way. But then they are apt to discover, upon checking the dictionary, that they are wrong.

Take the word "experiential." All logic would argue that this word should be spelled "experiencial" because it means that which is derived from experience. Yet the correct spelling is to use a *t* instead of a *c.*

So after you've pronounced the word, relied on memory devices, searched your mind for relevant rules, and pictured the word in your mind, *don't try to reason the spelling out anymore.* Just go with your first impression of what *seems* to be right, and the chances are you *will* be right.

6. Stay humble.

Very few people are potential spelling champs, and so most of us make egregious mistakes every now and then. Consequently, even as you become a significantly better speller (as I'm confident you will), it's unwise to allow even the semblance of arrogance to creep into your attitude. If you do, you're sure to fall on your face at some point.

I remember bragging to my wife about what an excellent speller I was becoming. "Sometimes, I get the feeling that given a few moments to reflect, I could spell almost any word that's worth spelling."

"How about 'restaurateur'?" she asked.

"What?"

" 'Restaurateur.' That's a word I've come across in a lot of reviews and restaurant magazines. How would you spell it?"

I suspected the problem was in the last syllable: *eur* or *uer*? And I knew the answer to that. So I quickly spelled, "R-E-S-T-A-U-R-A-N-T-E-U-R."

Wrong! I had relied on logic—I had reasoned that the spelling must include the word "restaurant." By inserting that *n* I had failed the test.

Though I was deflated, I did feel a little better when I consulted the dictionary. (*Always* check the dictionary after a humiliation!) There I learned that even though "restaurateur" was the preferred spelling, "restauranteur" was an alternate. Still, I had to admit that if the big restaurant magazines and reviewers were dropping the *n,* I should do likewise. Otherwise, I would risk possible criticism from those more knowledgeable than I about the restaurant business.

Humility is *always* the best policy when it comes to spelling, because if you don't make a mistake with one word, it's almost inevitable that you will with another. Here are two surefire ways to maintain your humility *and* be right:

• *When in doubt, check the dictionary*. That's not always possible, especially when you're asked to draft something on the spot. But it's always better to take a little extra time and be sure about a questionable word than to be wrong and end up with alphabet soup on your face.

A computer alternative is the "spelling check" feature now available on many word processors. Those who have access to this feature can check the spelling and punctuation for an entire letter or manuscript. But there are some limitations with this approach, including the failure of many spelling programs to include technical words or to identify the misuse or confusion of correctly spelled words. For example, the spelling checker may indicate that the word "there" is spelled correctly, but you may have meant "their."

• *Feel free to ask a colleague if you're not sure.* There's absolutely nothing wrong with saying, "Is there one *s* or two in 'occasion'?" With this approach, you do confess your ignorance. But you also demonstrate that you know there's an issue with the spelling of a particular word. Taking a chance and being wrong is a much worse alternative.

7. Make sure you've chosen the right word.

In the following pages, I've lumped word confusions—such as "antidote" and "anecdote," or "callous" and "callus"—with misspellings. Many of these confusions involve words technically known as "homophones," or those that sound alike but have different meanings and spellings. You don't have to worry about the academic distinctions. Just be aware that in many cases you have to be sure you've selected the right word before you can even consider how to spell it.

Now, let's move on to some of the specifics of effective spelling. You may feel you're terrible now, but you've embarked on a journey that will surely improve your expertise. The first stop in this little trip is to dispose of what I've called the "Toughest 228" words to spell.

2
The Toughest 228—
and How to Master Them

If you had the time and energy, you might become one of the best spellers in the world simply by memorizing all the entries in a good dictionary. But I don't know anyone who has this luxury.

A more efficient, if less comprehensive, method is first to identify a manageable, limited number of commonly used *and* misspelled words. Then, in a reasonable amount of time, you can memorize the spellings of those words cold. This is the approach that I propose to take in this chapter.

I've noted about 228 words that are used frequently in daily personal and business communication—and that are often misspelled. If you learn to master these "Toughest 228," you'll be well on your way to becoming a superior speller.

Each of the Toughest 228 entries is spelled correctly in alphabetical order. After the word, you'll find a brief discussion of how it's usually misspelled and also a suggested way to fix the correct spelling in your memory. For ease of reference, I've established a format for each entry: The first paragraph, beginning with "This word," states the meaning and common misspellings or misuses. The second paragraph, beginning with "You can remember," suggests mnemonic devices. Many of the mnemonic devices involve absurd associations or mental pictures. If you don't like mine, feel free to try your own! After all, the main purpose here is to remember the proper spellings.

ACCELERATE

This word, which means to cause something or someone to move faster or to happen at an earlier time, is most often misspelled by leaving out a *c* or adding an extra *l*.

You can remember the correct spelling this way: Imagine that as you walk down a highway, you are passed by a speeding stalk of celery. You first exclaim, "Ac!" Then you say, "Celery!"

ACCOMMODATE

This word, which means to produce agreement or to make someone or something suitable, is most often misspelled by dropping a *c* or an *m*.

You can remember the correct spelling this way: You see an unusual (or dirty) toilet and exclaim, "Ac! Commode!"

ACKNOWLEDGEABLE

This word, which means able to be recognized as having certain rights or status, is most often misspelled by omitting the *e* after the *g*.

You can remember the correct spelling by mispronouncing the end of the word: "-*gee*-able!"

Note: When you use the related noun, either "acknowledgment" or "acknowledgement" is acceptable, though "acknowledgment" is preferred in the American publishing community and the alternate spelling is likely to be *perceived* as an error.

ADDRESS

This word, which means to communicate directly or write directions for delivery, is most often misspelled by omitting a *d*.

You can remember the correct spelling this way: Think of an *ad*vertisement for a *dress*.

ADVERSE

This word, which refers to something or someone that *acts* or *is positioned against* something or someone else, is most often misspelled by dropping the *d*. (See the word "averse," which refers to a *feeling* of distaste or repugnance.)

You can remember the correct spelling this way: You may want to "*adver*tise" your intentions when you want to act against someone else, or take an opposite position.

AFFECT

This word, which means to influence, is most often misspelled (or the subject of word confusion) by substituting an *e* for the *a*. (The word "effect" means "result" when it's used as a noun, or "to bring about" when it's used as a verb.)

You can remember the correct spelling this way: Always pronounce "affect" with a clear *a* when you want to express the meaning "to influence."

ALL READY
This word—which means completely prepared, or which refers to every one of a group of people or items being prepared—is most often misspelled by turning it into one word, "already." (The word "already" means by this time.)

You can remember the correct spelling this way: If you want to indicate readiness, just think, "They are *all* ready."

ALL RIGHT
This word, which means satisfactory or pleasing, may be spelled "alright," according to most dictionaries. But the preferred spelling is "all right," and many people who are accustomed to formal English may assume you've made a mistake if you use "alright."

You can remember the preferred spelling this way: Think, "The cars *all* turned *right.*"

ALLUSION
This word, which means an implied or indirect reference, is most often misspelled as (or confused with) "illusion." (An illusion is something that misleads or deceives.)

You can remember the correct spelling this way: You only use "illusion" when you're referring to something that has an "ill," or negative, impact because it's misleading.

A LOT
This expression, which refers colloquially to a large amount, is most often misspelled by making it one word ("alot").

You can remember the correct spelling this way: There is no such word as "alot"! Also, when you're writing formal English, as in a business report, it's best to avoid "a lot" unless you're referring to a plot of land. Instead, use "a great deal" or some similar alternative.

ANECDOTE

This word, which means a short, illustrative story or narrative, is most often misspelled by dropping the *c* or by misusing the word "antidote." (An antidote is a remedy or solution.)

You can remember the correct spelling this way: Pronounce the syllable "nec" clearly—and think of craning your *nec*k to hear a good story.

ANOINT

This word, which means to bathe or rub with oil, is most often misspelled by adding an extra *n*.

You can remember the correct spelling this way: An anointing—such as in a royal or religious ceremony—is usually "*a no*-lose" situation.

ANTIDOTE

This word, which means a remedy, is most often misspelled by confusing it with "anecdote," which means a short story or narrative.

You can remember the correct spelling this way: A remedy is used *against*—or "*anti*"—a disease or poison.

APPARENT

This word, which means obvious, is most often misspelled by using the incorrect ending *ant*.

You can remember the correct spelling this way: "Apparent" is one word that has a "parent."

APPRAISE

This word, which means to estimate or place a value upon, is most often misspelled by confusing it with one of two other words, "apprise" or the less commonly used "apprize." ("Apprise" means to inform or give notice; "apprize" means to appreciate or value.)

You can remember the correct spelling this way: Reserve your *praise* for an expensively *appraised* house.

APPRISE

This word, which means to inform or give notice, is most often misspelled by confusing it with "appraise" or "apprize."

You can remember the correct spelling this way: Exaggerate the pronunciation to remind you of the spelling by saying "app-rr-eye-sss!"

AVERSE

This word, which refers to a *feeling* of distaste or repugnance, is most often misspelled by adding a *d* after the *a*. (Remember, "adverse" refers to or describes something or someone that *acts* or *is positioned against* something or someone else.)

You can remember the correct spelling this way: *A verse* of bad poetry may give you a feeling of distaste or repugnance.

BADMINTON

This word, which refers to a racket game played with a shuttlecock, is most often misspelled by dropping the *n* and putting in two *t*'s.

You can remember the correct spelling this way: To play this sport well, your racket must be in "mint" condition.

BAPTISM

This word, which means the act of purifying or cleansing (usually in a religious ceremony with water), is most often misspelled by substituting a *z* for the *s*. Also, sometimes a *b* is substituted incorrectly for the *p*. (The verb "baptize" *is* spelled with a *z*, a fact that makes remembering this spelling more difficult.)

You can remember the correct spelling this way: The *p* is necessary to remind you that you "*p*lunge" into the water (or that it's "*p*oured," depending on the method of baptism). You can remember the *ism* by remembering that many belief systems that require baptism (such as Methodism and Presbyterianism) end in *ism*.

BAPTIZE

This word, which means to purify or cleanse, usually in a religious ceremony with water, is most often misspelled by substituting an *s* for the *z*. Also, sometimes a *b* is substituted incorrectly for the *p*. (The British spelling for this word is "baptise." But as indicated above, the correct spelling for the noun is "baptism"—a fact that helps to confuse things further.)

You can remember the correct American spelling of the verb this way: As indicated under "baptism," allow the *p* to remind you that you "*p*lunge" into the water, or that the water is "*p*oured," depending on the method of baptism. The *z* in the verb can be remembered by overemphasizing the *z* in the pronunciation.

BEIGE

This word, which means a light grayish-brown or yellowish-brown color, is often misspelled by reversing the first *e* and the *i*, or by inserting an *a* for the first *e*.

You can remember the correct spelling this way: When you're writing, mispronounce the word as "beej," with an emphasis on the long *e* sound.

BIZARRE

This word, which means highly unusual, eccentric, or odd, is most often misspelled by confusing it with "bazaar," a market consisting of stalls selling a wide variety of goods. A variety of mistakes may occur, such as "bizaar," "bizaare," "bizzare," and "bazaar."

You can remember the correct spelling this way: When you write the word, mispronounce it by emphasizing the *z*, by rolling your *r*'s, and by adding a long *e* sound at the end: "bizzzarrreeee."

BRETHREN

This word, which means brothers or a group of men related by blood or commitment, is most often misspelled by adding an extra *e* after the *h*.

You can remember the correct spelling this way: Think of *thre*e brothers.

BURGLAR
This word, which means a thief who breaks into a dwelling or building, is often misspelled by adding an unnecessary *u* after the *g*, making "burgular." Sometimes it is misspelled by substituting an *e* for the *a*, making "burgler."

You can remember the correct spelling this way: Pronounce the word with only two syllables and with an emphasis on the *a* in the second syllable.

BUSINESS
This word, which refers to assigned activity, work, or things to do, is most often misspelled by dropping the *i*.

You can remember the correct spelling this way: Think of business as involving activity that keeps you busy—and remember that "busy" is included in the spelling, with the *i* substituted for the *y*.

CAFFEINE
This word, which refers to the stimulating chemical found in coffee and tea, is most often misspelled by dropping the final *e*. Also, a mistake may be made by reversing the *e* and *i* or by substituting an extra *e* for the *i*.

You can remember the correct spelling this way: First, remind yourself that coffee ends *in* two *e*'s. Then, to get the correct spelling, you just have to insert an *in* between the two *e*'s in "caffeine."

CALENDAR

This word, which refers to the dates in the year or an orderly list of events, is most often misspelled by substituting an *e* for the final *a*.

You can remember the correct spelling this way: In writing the word, mispronounce by overemphasizing the *a* in the final syllable.

CALLOUS

This word, which means being hardened or having no feeling toward others, is most often misspelled by omitting the *o*. (The word "callus" means a buildup of tough tissue on the feet or hands.)

You can remember the correct spelling this way: A callous person is a *louse*.

CALLUS

This word, which means a buildup of tough tissue on the feet or hands, is most often misspelled by adding an *o* before the *u*. (The word "callous" means being hardened or having no feeling toward others.)

You can remember the correct spelling this way: Think that a doctor might say "Call us" if the skin gets too tough for comfort.

CAMARADERIE

This word, which means friendly interaction between colleagues, is most often misspelled by dropping the second *a*, making "camraderie."

You can remember the correct spelling this way: Pronounce every syllable (though technically, it's acceptable to pronounce this word without the second syllable).

CAPITAL

This word, which means a city that is the seat of government, is most often misspelled by substituting an *o* for the second *a*. (The word "capitol" means the *building* where government is conducted.)

You can remember the correct spelling this way: Think, "We calculated the income in the *capital* per *capita* (per person)." Or you might think, "The capit*al* includes *all* the people in the city"—not just those who work for the government.

CAPITOL

This word, which means the building where government is conducted, is most often misspelled by substituting an *a* for the *o*. (The word "capital" means a city that is the seat of government. Also, the word is capitalized, "Capitol," when the meaning is the U.S. Capitol, which is the building that houses the national legislature.)

You can remember the correct spelling this way: A capit*ol* contains *o*nly the legislators.

CARIBBEAN

This word, which refers to the sea immediately southwest of Florida, is most often misspelled by adding an extra *r* and perhaps by dropping a *b*.

You can remember the correct spelling this way: This sea contains a "rib" and a "bean."

CATEGORY
This word, which means a class established for a similar group of items or persons, is most often misspelled by substituting an *a* for the *e*.

You can remember the correct spelling this way: This word contains the word "ate."

CHOOSE
This word, which means to select or pick, is the present tense of the verb "to choose" and is most often misspelled by omitting an *o*. (The word "chose" is the past tense of the verb.)

You can remember the correct spelling this way: The present tense contains the first part of a child's train, a "choo-choo."

CHOSE
This word, which means to select or pick, is the past tense of the verb "to choose" and is most often misspelled by adding an extra *o*. (The word "choose" is the present tense of the verb.)

You can remember the correct spelling this way: The past tense of the verb contains a "hose."

CITE
This word, which means to call on a person in court or to refer to something or someone as an authority or exam-

ple, is most often misspelled by substituting an *s* for the *c*. (The word "site," though pronounced the same way, means a location or place.)

You can remember the correct spelling by noting that "cite," which begins with a *c*, means to *c*all on someone or something.

COLLABORATE

This word, which means to work together, is most often misspelled by dropping an *l*.

You can remember the correct spelling by noting that to work together, you need a *coll*eague.

COMPLEMENT

This word, which means that which completes or adds to something else, is most often misspelled by substituting an *i* for the first *e*. (The word "compliment" means an expression of respect or esteem.)

You can remember the correct spelling by noting that the word "com*ple*ment means that which com*ple*tes.

COMPLIMENT

This word, which means an expression of respect or esteem, is most often misspelled by substituting an *e* for the *i*. (The word "complement" means that which completes or adds to something else.)

You can remember the correct spelling by noting that the word "lime" is contained in "comp*lim*ent." Also, remember that this word does *not* mean "complete," and so the letters of "*comple*te" aren't included.

CONCEDE

This word, which means to grant or accept something as true, is most often misspelled by substituting an *s* for the second *c*.

You can remember the correct spelling by noting that there are two *c*'s in the word.

COROLLARY

This word, which means something that follows naturally from something else, is most often misspelled by adding an extra *r* after the first *r*, or dropping an *l*, or making both of these mistakes.

You can remember the correct spelling by mispronouncing the word as "co-roll-aree." Emphasize the "co" and the "roll."

COUNCIL

This word, which means a group that meets to give advice or consultation, is most often misspelled by substituting *se* for the *ci*. (The word "counsel," used as a verb, means to give advice. Used as a noun, it means the advice given or a lawyer who represents a party.)

You can remember the correct spelling by noting that the ending *cil* rhymes with "pencil," an instrument that is necessary for any group that is conducting a meeting.

COUNSEL

This word, when used as a verb, means to give advice. When used as a noun, it means advice given or a lawyer who represents a party. The word is most often misspelled by substituting *ci* for the *se*. (The word "council" means a group that meets to give advice or consultation.)

You can remember the correct spelling this way: Advice involves *s*aying something to someone else. Both "coun*s*el" and "*s*ay" contain an *s*.

CRITERION, CRITERIA

These words are often incorrectly used interchangeably. "Criterion" is the singular form, which means a standard or characterizing mark. "Criteria" is the plural, which means more than one standard or characterizing mark.

You can remember the correct spelling this way: "Criteri*on* involves *on*e point or item.

CURRICULUM, CURRICULA

Mistakes can be made with these words in several ways. First of all, they are often used interchangeably, but that's incorrect because "curriculum" (meaning a set of courses in an educational institution) is the singular, and "curricula" (meaning several sets of courses) is the plural.

Second, the words may be misspelled by dropping an *r* or by substituting an *i* for the first *u*.

You can remember the correct spelling by thinking that a *curr*iculum in a cooking school might impart information on the use of *curr*y. (For more detail on how to distinguish between the *um* and *a* endings, see the discussion of Latin in Chapter 4.)

DECEIVE

This word, which means to cause someone to accept as true something that is actually false, is most often misspelled by reversing the *e* and the *i*.

You can remember the correct spelling by noting that this word falls under the old rule: "*i* before *e* except after *c*." Also, words like "receive" and "deceive" tend to have the long *e* sound after the *c*, and that makes it easier to remember that the *e* follows the *c*.

DELUXE

This word, which means elegant or luxurious, is most often misspelled by dropping the final *e*.

You can remember the correct spelling by noting that anything that is delux*e* must be *e*xcellent.

DESERT

As a verb, this word means to leave or withdraw without approval and without intent to return. As a noun, it means a desolate or barren tract of land, *or* a reward or sanction that is deserved (as in "just deserts"). The word is most often misspelled by adding an extra *s*. (The word "dessert" means the final dish, often sweet, served at the end of a meal.)

You can remember the correct spelling by noting that there is often sand on a desert, and the word "*s*and" has only one *s*.

DESSERT

This word, which means the final dish, often sweet, served at the end of a meal, is most often misspelled by dropping an *s*.

You can remember the correct spelling this way: Sweets are often served for dessert, and the word "*s*weet*s*" has two *s*'s.

DISASSEMBLE
This word, which means to take apart, is often confused with "dissemble." (The word "dissemble" means to put on a false appearance.)

You can remember the correct spelling by taking the word apart: "dis-assemble." The word "assemble" must be present if the thing that has been assembled is to be broken down.

DISCREET
This word, which refers to the quality of showing good judgment, is most often misspelled by confusing it with "discrete." ("Discrete" means separate or distinct.)

You can remember the correct spelling this way: Those who are discr*eet* must watch where they go on their *feet*. Also, in "discrete," the *e*'s are separated by a *t*—and the meaning of "discrete" involves a form of separation. If there is no separation, the spelling must be "discreet."

DISCRETE
This word, which means being separate or distinct, is most often misspelled by confusing it with "discreet." ("Discreet" means showing good judgment.)

You can remember the correct spelling this way: In "discrete," the *e*'s are separated by a *t* (and remember that the meaning of "discrete" involves a form of separation). If there is no separation, the spelling must be "discreet."

DISSEMBLE

This word, which means to put on a false appearance, is most often misspelled by confusing it with "disassemble."

You can remember the correct spelling this way: Those who dis*sembl*e take on the *sembl*ance of something or someone else.

The distinction between "dissemble" and "disassemble" can become the acid test of good spelling—and in some instances, of an adequate educational background. I recall one book review in which the critic skewered the author because he used "dissemble" for "disassemble." In the reviewer's mind, everything else in the book was apparently suspect because of this one mistake!

I had my own uncomfortable encounter with these words while I was an undergraduate at Harvard. As the chairman of the Constitution Committee of the Freshman Council, I had the responsibility of posting proposed changes to the council's constitution in the Freshman Union, the dining hall for first-year students. Unfortunately, I used "dissemble" instead of "disassemble" in referring to the desire of my committee to take apart one section of the old document. Within hours, the posted proposals were covered with pointed—and rather unkind, I thought—gibes at my English ability.

DONOR

This word, which means one who gives something, is most often misspelled by substituting and *e* for the final *o*.

You can remember the correct spelling this way: Never say "*no*" to a do*no*r!

EFFECT

This word, which as a noun means result and as a verb means to bring about, is most often misspelled (when writing the verb) by substituting an *a* for the first *e*. (The word "affect" means to influence or to have an impact upon.)

You can remember the correct spelling this way: The verb "effect," which means to bring about or to cause to happen, should be linked to "effective," which means having the power to produce a certain happening or effect. Also, you might mispronounce this word with a long *e* to remind yourself that it begins with an *e*, not an *a*.

EMINENT

This word, which means noticeable, prominent, or of high standing, is most often misspelled by confusing it with "imminent," which means pending or about to happen.

You can remember the *e* in the correct spelling this way: An *e*minent person is one who is *e*xcellent in some way.

ENVELOP

This word, which is a verb that means to enclose, is most often misspelled by adding an *e* at the end. (The word "envelope" is a noun that means the paper container for a letter.)

You can remember the correct spelling this way: The ending for "envelop" is "lop," which means to cut off something. The last syllable of "envelop" and the verb "lop" are pronounced approximately the same way. The ending for "envelope" is "lope," which means to move along at an easy, bounding gait. The last syllable of "envelope" and the verb "lope" are pronounced the same way.

ENVELOPE

This word, which means the container for a letter, is most often misspelled by dropping the final *e*. (The word "envelop" means to enclose.)

You can remember the correct spelling as described under "envelop": The ending for "envelop" is "lop," which means to cut off something. The last syllable of "envelop" and the verb "lop" are pronounced about the same way. The ending for "envelope" is "lope," which means to move along at an easy, bounding gait. The last syllable of "envelope" and the verb "lope" are pronounced the same way.

ET CETERA

This word is a Latin phrase that means "and so forth" or "and others." It is most often misspelled "eckcetera," "etcetera," or "etcetra." (The confusion may stem in part from the fact that the abbreviation for "et cetera" is "etc.")

You can remember the correct spelling this way: Pronounce the two Latin words clearly, with a rest between the first and second word, and a clipped rendition of all three syllables in the second word.

EXCERPT

This word, which means a short passage selected from a longer work, is most often misspelled by dropping the *c*.

You can remember the correct spelling this way: Pronounce the word correctly, with a clear *s* sound for the *c*.

EXPERIENTIAL

This word, which means relating to or derived from experience, is most often misspelled by substituting a *c* for the *t*.

You can remember the correct spelling this way: Be illogical. The logical way to spell the word would be with a *c* because that's the way "experience" is spelled. So in this case, do the illogical thing and use a *t*.

FARTHEST

This word, which means to the most distant point, is most often misspelled "fartherest," probably because the word "farther" is the root.

You can remember the correct spelling this way: Pronounce the word correctly, with only two syllables, not three.

FIERY

This word, which means covered with or made up of fire, is most often misspelled "firey."

You can remember the correct spelling this way: Emphasize the alternate pronunciation, which involves three syllables: "fi-e-ry."

FILIPINO

This word, which means a native or citizen of the Philippines, is most often misspelled "Philippino" or "Philipino."

You can remember the correct spelling—with an initial *F* and one *p*—this way: *F*ili*p*inos live *f*ar across the *P*acific.

FLORESCENT
This word, which means flourishing, blossoming, or blooming, is most often misspelled by adding a *u* before the *o*. (The word "fluorescent" means glowing brightly as a result of the emission of electromagnetic radiation, as does a fluorescent lamp.)

You can remember the correct spelling this way: That which is *flo*rescent should remind you of a *flo*wer.

FLUORESCENT
This word, which means glowing brightly as a result of the emission of electromagnetic radiation, is most often misspelled by dropping the *u*.

You can remember the correct spelling this way: That which is *flu*orescent will il*lu*minate a room.

FORBEAR
This word, which means to hold back, avoid, or leave alone, is most often misspelled by adding an *e* before the *b*. (The word "forebear" means ancestor.)

You can remember the correct spelling this way: In the woods, the best response *for bear* is to avoid them or leave them alone.

FOREBEAR
This word, which means ancestor, is most often misspelled by adding an *er* at the end. (An alternate spelling

of "forebear" is "forbear," though "forebear" is preferred.)

You can remember the correct spelling this way: There
are only two syllables in "forebear."

FORSYTHIA

This word, which refers to plants with yellow, bell-shaped
flowers that bloom in early spring, is most often misspelled by substituting a *c* for the *s*, or by substituting an
i for the *y*.

You can remember the correct spelling this way: For-
*sy*thias appear in the *s*pring and are *y*ellow.

FORTE

This word, which may mean either a strong point or a loud
passage in a piece of music, is most often misspelled by
dropping the *e*. Also, the words should be pronounced
correctly: If the meaning is strong point, the final *e* isn't
sounded; it's pronounced just like the word "fort." But if
the musical term is intended, the final *e* is sounded as a
long *a*—"for-tay."

You can remember the correct spelling this way: Only
the strong building is spelled "fort." The other spellings
are always "forte."

As for the pronunciation, remember when the meaning
of "forte" is strong point, the word is sounded exactly like
the strong building ("fort"). But when the term is used
musically, the pronunciation is more "foreign," with the
final *e* being sounded.

FULFILL

This word, which means to satisfy or to measure up, is most often misspelled by adding an extra *l* after the first *l*. (An alternate spelling is "fulfil," though "fulfill" is preferred.)

You can remember the correct spelling this way: The only double *l* that's allowed in this word must come *after* a single *l*.

FULFILLMENT

This word, which means the state of being satisfied or of measuring up, is most often misspelled by adding an extra *l* after the first *l*. (An alternate spelling in some dictionaries is "fulfilment.")

You can remember the correct spelling this way: The only double *l* that's allowed must come after the single *l*.

FURTHEST

This word, which means the most advanced in degree or extent, is most often misspelled "furtherest."

You can remember the correct spelling this way: There are only two syllables in this word—even though its root is the word "further."

GRAMMAR

This word, which means the principles and study of proper word usage and function in a language, is most often misspelled by substituting an *e* for the final *a*.

You can remember the correct spelling this way: Mispronounce the word by emphasizing the *a* in the final syllable: "ahhhrrr."

GRIEVOUS
This word, which means causing great pain or grief, is most often misspelled by adding an *i* before the *o*.

You can remember the correct spelling this way: There are only two syllables in the word when it's properly pronounced "gree-vus." Keeping this fact in mind will prevent you from sounding it out erroneously as "gree-vee-us."

GUARANTEE
This word, which carries the primary meaning of an assurance that a certain commitment or condition will be fulfilled, is most often misspelled by dropping the *u*. Also, the word "guaranty" is sometimes used synonymously with "guarantee" to convey the above meaning, even though "guarantee" is the preferred word.

You can remember the correct spelling this way: A *guar*antee involves an ass*u*rance of performance. Also, it may help to mispronounce the *guar* as "goo-ahrr."

GUARANTY
This word carries the primary meaning of an undertaking to answer for the performance of or payment by another party (as with one who cosigns a note of debt). It's most often misspelled by dropping the *u*. Also, it may be used synonymously with "guarantee," even though "guaranty" in this case would be the preferred word.

You can remember the correct spelling by mispronouncing the word, as with "guarantee": Say the *guar* as "goo-ahrr."

HAIL
This word, which may mean small balls or droplets of ice from the sky, or a greeting or exclamation, is most often misspelled by confusing it with "hale," which means healthy.

You can remember the correct spelling this way: Ha*i*l involves *i*ce. Also, this "*hai*l, which means a greeting, contains the greeting "*hi*."

Note: The phrase "hail-fellow-well-met" requires this kind of "hail."

HALE
This word, which means healthy, is most often misspelled by confusing it with "hail," which means droplets of ice or a greeting.

You can remember the correct spelling this way: This healthy "h*ale*" contains an "*ale*," but not any "*ail*ment."

HANDKERCHIEF
This word, which means a small piece of cloth used for personal purposes such as nose-blowing, is most often misspelled by dropping the *d.*

You can remember the correct spelling this way: Mispronounce the word by saying "hand" clearly as you write.

HANDYMAN

This word, which means a person who does odd jobs, is most often misspelled by substituting an *i* for the *y* or by turning it into two words.

You can remember the correct spelling this way: The word describes someone who is handy (not "handi"). Also, picture "Handyman" as a one-word name for a person in a cape who represents a kind of odd-job Superman.

HANGAR

This word, which means the shelter used to house and repair aircraft, is most often misspelled by substituting an *e* for the second *a*. (The word "hanger" means a person who hangs something, or a device used to hang other things on.)

You can remember the correct spelling this way: A han-g*ar* is used for *a*ircraft.

HANGER

This word, which means a person who hangs something, or a device used to hang other things on, is most often misspelled by substituting an *a* for the *e*. (The word "hangar" means the housing shed for aircraft.)

You can remember the correct spelling this way: This kind of hanger does *not* involve *a*ircraft, so there is no *a*.

HARASS

This word, which means to worry or annoy, is most often misspelled by adding an extra *r*.

You can remember the correct spelling this way: Think of a laugh and a cheer, *"Ha-ra*h."

HEMORRHAGE

This word, which means heavy bleeding, often internally, is most often misspelled by adding an extra *m*, by dropping an *r*, or by omitting the second *h*.

You can remember the correct spelling this way: Mispronounce the word to emphasize the proper spelling. You might say, "Hee-moh-rrrr-hage." Also, you might note that the words "he" and "hag" and the beginning of the name *"Morris"* are contained in this word.

HOMICIDE

Even many lawyers can't spell this word, which means the killing of one person by another, or the person who does the killing. The word is most often misspelled by substituting the letter *o* for the first *i*.

You can remember the correct spelling this way: The two *i*'s in homicide are necessary to remind us that *killing* is involved.

HYGIENE

This word, which means the study or practice of cleanliness and health, is most often misspelled by substituting an *i* for the *y*, or by dropping the *i* after *g*.

You can remember the correct spelling this way: If you see a very dirty, disease-infested place, you might exclaim, *"Yi*ke! This needs *hygi*ene!"

HYPOCRISY

This word, which means pretending to be what you're not, is most often misspelled by substituting an *i* for the first *y*, or by substituting an *a* for the *i*.

You can remember the correct spelling this way: As with "hygiene," think "*Yi*ke!" if you encounter an obvious hypoc*ri*te.

ILLUSION

This word, which means something that misleads or deceives, is most often misspelled as "allusion." (The word "allusion" means an implied or indirect reference.)

You can remember the correct spelling this way: Only use "*ill*usion" when you're referring to something that has an "*ill*" effect because it's misleading.

IMMANENT

This word, which means operating in something else, or existing in the mind rather than the outside world, is most often misspelled as "imminent" or "eminent." ("Imminent" means hanging over, or about to occur; "eminent" means prominent.)

You can remember the correct spelling this way: That which is *imma*nent is *i*nside *a*nother person or thing.

IMMINENT

This word, which means hanging over, or about to occur, is most often misspelled as "immanent" or "eminent." (The word "immanent" means operating in something else, or existing in the mind rather than the outside world; "eminent" means prominent.)

You can remember the correct spelling this way: That which is im*min*ent may happen in the next *min*ute.

INACCESSIBLE

This word, which means not accessible or available, may be misspelled several ways: "unacessible," "inaccesible," or most common of all, "inaccessable."

You can remember the correct spelling by breaking the word down into three sections and memorizing each: "in," which means "not"; "access"; and "ible." You can remember the *ible* ending by mispronouncing this ending to emphasize the *i*.

INADMISSIBLE

This word, which means not admissible, is most often misspelled by substituting an *a* for the final *i*.

You can remember the correct spelling this way: There is a *missile* in inad*missi*ble.

INCONCEIVABLE

This word, which means unable to be comprehended or believed, is most often misspelled by substituting an *s* for the second *c*; by putting the second *i* before the *e*; or by ending it in *ible*.

You can remember the correct spelling by breaking the word down into three parts: (1) "in," which means "not." (2) "conceiv." Here, just remember there are two *c*'s and no *s*'s in the word. Also, remember that the placement of *e* before *i* is consistent with the old rule "*i* before *e* except after *c*. (3) "able." Believing a f*able* is inconceiv*able*.

INDEFENSIBLE

This word, which means incapable of being justified or protected, is most often misspelled by substituting a *c* for the *s* or by ending it in *able*.

You can remember the correct spelling this way: The word "*in*defen*sible*" contains most of the letters of "*sibling*."

INDISPENSABLE

This word, which means essential or absolutely necessary, is most often misspelled "indespensable," "indispensible," or "indispencible."

You can remember the correct spelling by breaking the word down into four parts. (1) "in," which means "not." (2) "dis," which may remind you of "Disney." (3) "pens." (4) "able." This ending should be mispronounced to emphasize the *a*.

INEDIBLE

This word, which means not fit to be eaten, is most often misspelled as "inedable," "inetible" or "inetable."

You can remember the correct spelling this way: In mulling over that which is in*edi*ble, think, it would be unpleasant to *e*at a *d*ish of *i*nsects.

INNOCUOUS

This word, which means harmless or producing no injury, is most often misspelled by omitting one *n*.

You can remember the correct spelling this way: Think *in*jure *no*t!

INOCULATE
This word, which means to introduce a microorganism into the body to treat or prevent a disease, is most often misspelled by adding an extra *n*.

You can remember the correct spelling this way: Think, "*I* k*no*c*k* yo*u*."

INTERCEDE
This word, which means to mediate, or intervene in order to reconcile differences, is most often misspelled by spelling it "intersede" or "interceed."

You can remember the correct spelling this way: Think "*cer*tificate of *de*posit."

ISAIAH
This word, which comes from the name of the ancient Hebrew prophet and is also the name of a book of the Bible, is most often misspelled by dropping an *a*.

You can remember the correct spelling by mispronouncing the word to add an *i* sound: "eye-say-eye-ah."

ISRAEL
This word, which refers to the Middle Eastern nation and also the alternate name of the ancient Hebrew patriarch Jacob, is most often misspelled "Isreal."

You can remember the correct spelling this way: Pronounce it with a heavy emphasis on the *a* and then the *el*.

Also, it helps to recall that one of the Hebrew words for God is "el." (The word "Israel" means literally "let God contend.")

ITS

This word, which is the possessive of "it" (that is, the word indicates that "it" owns something), is most often misspelled by inserting an apostrophe before the *s*. (The word "it's" is a contraction of "it is.")

You can remember the correct spelling this way: With nouns, such as "John" or "apple," the possessive is formed by adding apostrophe-s. So, these would be written "John's" and "apple's." But with "it" the possessive is formed by adding an *s without* an apostrophe.

IT'S

This word, which is a shortened form (a contraction) of "it is," is most often misspelled by omitting the apostrophe. (The word "its" is the possessive form of "it.")

You can remember the correct spelling this way: All contractions have an apostrophe to indicate that a letter is missing.

JEWELRY

This word, which means objects of precious stones or metal that are worn as adornment, is most often misspelled by dropping the second *e*.

You can remember the correct spelling by pronouncing the word correctly, with all three syllables.

JOIE DE VIVRE

This word, which comes directly from the French and means "joy of living," may be misspelled in a number of ways, such as "joy de vivre," "joi de viver," "joi de vivre," or "joie de viver."

You can remember the correct spelling by mispronouncing the word to emphasize the correct letters (unless you speak French, in which case the spelling should come easily).

KEOGH

This word, which refers to a pension plan for self-employed people (a Keogh Plan), is most often misspelled by adding a *u* before the *g*.

You can remember the correct spelling by mispronouncing the word: "Key-og-h."

KINDERGARTEN

This word, which means a school or class for young children in the year before first grade, is most often misspelled by substituting a *d* for the *t*.

You can remember the correct spelling this way: Every kindergarten must have a teacher.

LABORATORY

This word, which means a place set aside for experimentation and specialized study, is most often misspelled by dropping the first *o*.

You can remember the correct spelling this way: A *lab-*

*or*atory involves *labor* by a specialist. Also, be sure to pronounce every syllable.

LED
This word, which is the past tense or past participle of the verb "to lead," is most often mixed up with "lead," the present tense of "to lead." Also, "lead" (pronounced just like "led") is the heavy metal

You can remember the correct spelling this way: The word "led" is used only as the past tense or past participle of "to lead." Also, "lead" as a verb is only used to express present actions of "to lead."

LESSOR
This word, which means one who conveys property by a lease, is most often misspelled by substituting an *e* for the *o*. (The word "lesser" describes something that is of smaller or less significance than something else.)

You can remember the correct spelling this way: Pronounce the word by emphasizing the *or*.

LIABLE
This word, which means responsible or obligated under law, is most often misspelled as "libel." (The word "libel" means a written statement that defames someone else.)

You can remember the correct spelling this way: Pronounce all three syllables.

LIBEL
This word, which refers to a written statement that defames someone else, is most often misspelled as "liable."

(The word "liable" means responsible or obligated under law.)

You can remember the correct spelling this way: Pronounce only two syllables.

LIGHTNING

This word, which means the flashing of light produced by a discharge of electricity in the atmosphere, is most often misspelled by adding an *e* before the first *n*. (The word "lightening" refers to a reduction in a load of weight or an increased use of lighter colors in a picture.)

You can remember the correct spelling this way: Pronounce only two syllables.

LIMOUSINE

This word, which means a large and luxurious automobile, often driven by a chauffeur, is most often misspelled by omitting the *u*.

You can remember the correct spelling this way: Imagine a li*mous*ine for a *mouse*.

MASSACHUSETTS

This word, which refers to the New England state, is most often misspelled by substituting a *t* for the *ch*. Also, sometimes one of the final *t*'s is dropped.

You can remember the correct spelling this way: Pronounce the word correctly, with an emphasis on the syllable *chu*. As for the final *t*'s, think in terms of the early *sett*lers who came to Massachu*sett*s.

MAYONNAISE

This word, which refers to a fatty food dressing made of eggs, vegetable oil, and vinegar, is most often misspelled by dropping an *n,* by dropping the *i,* or by adding an extra *s* between *s* and *e.*

You can remember the correct spelling by breaking the word up into three parts and mispronouncing it accordingly: "ma," "yonna," "ise."

MEDAL

This word, which means a metal piece that is given as an award or commemoration, is most often misspelled as "metal." (The word "metal" refers to the hard, opaque substance used for building and other purposes.)

You can remember the correct spelling this way: A me*d*al is an awar*d.*

MEDITERRANEAN

This word, which refers to the great sea that lies just south of Europe and north of Africa, is most often misspelled by omitting an *r* or adding an extra *n* after the first *n.*

You can remember the correct spelling by breaking the word down into three parts: "Medi," which comes from a Latin word, *medius,* meaning "middle"; "terra," which comes from the Latin meaning "land"; and "nean."

MEMENTO

This word, which means something that reminds, or a souvenir, is often spelled "momento." Though "momento" is accepted as correct by some dictionaries, "memento" is preferred.

You can remember the preferred spelling this way: A *mem*ento conjures up a *mem*ory.

METAL

This word, which means the hard, opaque, inorganic substances used for so many purposes, is most often misspelled by substituting a *d* for the *t*. (The word "medal" means a metal piece that is given as an award or commemoration.)

You can remember the correct spelling this way: Me*t*al is a *t*ough material.

MILLENNIUM

This word, which means a period of 1,000 years, is most often misspelled by dropping an *l* or an *n* or both.

You can remember the correct spelling by breaking the word down into two parts: "mill," which comes from the Latin word *mille*, meaning 1,000; and "ennium," which comes from the Latin *anni*, meaning years.

Don't be frightened of these references to the Latin roots. As you'll see in Chapter 4, you don't have to be a Latin scholar to take advantage of the language in your spelling. In this case, keeping the Latin in mind will help you remember that "millennium" is rooted in Latin words that have two *l*'s and two *n*'s.

MISSILE

This word, which means an object that is projected or thrown into the air toward a target, is most often misspelled as "missle" or "missal." (The word "missal" means a book containing all the annual readings and songs for church mass.)

You can remember the correct spelling this way: Use the British pronunciation for the second *i*. This involves a long *i* sound (as in "eye") for the second *i*.

MISSPELL

This word, which means to spell incorrectly, is most often misspelled by dropping an *s* or an *l*.

You can remember the correct spelling this way: The word contains the smaller words "miss" and "spell," though the last *s* in "miss" overlaps with the first *s* in "spell."

MURMUR

This word, which means to utter low, nearly inaudible sounds in a continuous manner, is most often misspelled by substituting an *e* for the final *u*.

You can remember the correct spelling this way: Think of the reverse spelling for this word, which is "rumrum."

NAVAL

This word, which means relating to a navy, is most often misspelled by substituting an *e* for the second *a*. (The word "navel" refers to the mark on the abdomen left when the umbilical cord is cut at birth.)

You can remember the correct spelling this way: To remember the *a* think "*a*nchors *a*weigh."

NAVEL

This word, which means the mark left on the abdomen when the umbilical cord is cut at birth, is most often misspelled by substituting an *a* for the *e*. (The word "naval" means relating to the navy.)

You can remember the correct spelling this way: A na-v*e*l can be found on *e*verybody.

NICOTINE

This word, which refers to the poisonous chemical in tobacco, is often misspelled by making an error in the ending, such as "nicotein" or "nicoteen."

You can remember the correct spelling this way: Think, nico*tine* contains "tin" plus an *e*.

NINETY

This word, which means the number equal to nine tens, is often misspelled by dropping the *e*.

You can remember the correct spelling this way: The word "ninety" must contain "nine."

NON SEQUITUR

This phrase, which is the Latin for "it does not follow," means an inference that doesn't follow from given assumptions. It is most often misspelled by writing it as one word, "nonsequitur," by substituting an *a* for the *i*, or by substituting an *e* or an *o* for the final *u*.

You can remember the correct spelling this way: First, note that there are *two* Latin words. Next, you can see that the word "quit" is present. Finally, mispronounce the *ur* as "you-are."

NOTICEABLE

This word, which means able to be or worthy of being noticed, is most often misspelled by dropping the first *e*. Also, the ending may be written incorrectly as *ible*.

You can remember the correct spelling this way: Mispronounce the word by emphasizing the *e* that is likely to be omitted: "noh-tis-*see*-able." As for the ending, remember that the word "notice*able*" means *able* to be noticed.

OCCASION

This word, which means a favorable opportunity or a condition that brings something about, is most often misspelled by dropping a *c* or adding an *s*.

You can remember the correct spelling this way: Think, "see-see-s (ccs)." By focusing on these three letters, you should get the spelling right.

OCCURRENCE

This word, which means an event or a happening, is most often misspelled by omitting a *c*, omitting an *r*, or ending the word in *ance*. (Note: The word "occur" is spelled with two *c*'s but only one *r*, while "occurring" and "occurred" have two *r*'s.)

You can remember the correct spelling this way: First, think double *c* and double *r*. Then, the fact that an occurrence is an *e*vent should remind you of the *ence* ending.

OFFENSE

This word, which means something that outrages one's sensibilities, or an act of attacking another, is most often misspelled by dropping an *f*. The spelling "offence" is acceptable, though the preferred spelling is "offense."

You can remember the preferred spelling this way: An *off*ense can tick you *off*.

OPHTHALMOLOGY

This word, which means the branch of medical practice dealing with the eyes, may be misspelled in a variety of ways, including the following: "opthalmology," "ophthamology," "opthamology," and "opthamalogy."

You can remember the correct spelling by being very careful about the correct pronunciation. Sound out each syllable and letter: "oph-thal-mol-o-gy." Note that in the first syllable, the *ph* is pronounced like an *f*.

PAGEANT

This word, which means a showy display, may be misspelled in several ways: "pajeant," "pagent," "pagant," "pagaent," or "pageunt."

You can remember the correct spelling this way: "Pageant" contains two words, "page" and "ant."

PALATE

This word, which means the roof of the mouth or the center of taste, is most often misspelled by confusing it with "palette" or "pallet." ("Palette" means a tablet or board used by a painter to mix and hold colors, while "pallet" means a small hard mattress, or a wooden platform used to move material in a warehouse.)

You can remember the correct spelling this way: You use your *palate* to taste food served on a *plate*.

PALETTE

This word, which means a tablet or board used by a painter to mix and hold colors, is most often misspelled by confusing it with "palate" or "pallet." (The word "palate" means the roof of the mouth or the center of taste; the word "pallet" means a small hard mattress, or a wooden platform used to move material in a warehouse.)

You can remember how to spell "palette" in a couple of ways. First, the ending *ette* has a "French art" sound that the other spellings lack. Second, think that the proper use of a *palette* helps you achieve a *pale tincture*, or *pale tint*.

PALLET

This word, which means a small hard mattress or a wooden platform used to move material in a warehouse, is most often misspelled by confusing it with "palate" or "palette." ("Palate" means the roof of the mouth or the center of taste. "Palette" means a tablet or board used by a painter to mix and hold colors.)

You can remember the correct spelling this way: A *pallet* is helpful when a *pal lets* you sleep on his floor.

PARI-MUTUEL

This word, which refers to a system of sharing the winnings on horse race betting, is most often misspelled by substituting an *a* for the *i* or an *a* for the *e*.

You can remember the correct spelling this way: Remember the word "pari-mutuel" contains the word "rim" and ends unexpectedly—as horse races are wont to do—in *el*.

PARLIAMENT

This word, which refers to the main legislative body in many countries, is most often misspelled by omitting the *i* or the second *a*.

You can remember the correct spelling by mispronouncing the word: "par-lee-ah-ment."

PART-TIME

This word, which means working fewer than the standard number of hours, is most often misspelled by omitting the hyphen and dropping a *t*.

You can remember the correct spelling this way: Think in terms of two words: "part" and "time"—and just memorize the fact that they are joined by a hyphen.

PASTIME

This word, which means an activity that helps the time pass in a positive way, is most often misspelled by adding an extra *t* and perhaps joining the two parts of the word by a hyphen.

You can remember the correct spelling this way: Think of the word as meaning something to "*pass time*." This way, you'll be less likely to insert an extra *t* or a hyphen.

PENULTIMATE

This word, which means next to the last, is often misspelled by substituting an *i* for the first *e*. Also, the word is frequently used or defined incorrectly as the ultimate or last, rather than the next to last.

You can remember the correct spelling by thinking in terms of these two words: "pen" and "ultimate." Also, the word sounds like *"peanut."*

PERENNIAL
This word, which means being present during all seasons of the year, or being constant, is most often misspelled by adding an extra *r* or dropping an *n*.

You can remember the correct spelling by dividing the word into two parts: "per," which is the Latin word meaning "through," and "ennial," which comes from the Latin word *anni* meaning years (see the discussion of "millennium").

Another memory device that may help you recall the two *n*'s and one *r* is to think that this word involves things that happen for a*nn*ual *per*iods.

PERMANENCE
This word, which means the state of being permanent, is most often misspelled by ending it in *ance*.

You can remember the correct spelling this way: There is a *mane* in per*mane*nce.

PHENOMENON
This word, which means an event or object known through the senses, or an exceptional event or person, may be misspelled in many ways, including the following: "phe-

nomenum," "fenomenon," phinomenon," "phemonenon," "phenominon," or "phenomonon."

I've always had trouble with this word, especially when I try to write it quickly. It's all too easy to put the letters in the wrong places. But I've managed to spell it correctly with some consistency using this method: I mispronounce the word by exaggerating the sound of the vowels: "fee-no-me-non."

PHILIPPINES

This word, which refers to that island nation in the Pacific Ocean, is most often misspelled by adding an extra *l* or omitting one of the last two *p*'s.

You can remember the correct spelling by breaking the word down into three parts: "Phi," "lip," and "pines." You'll note that this approach identifies two smaller words, "lip" and "pines." The first part, "Phi," which is the twenty-first letter of the Greek alphabet, will be easy to remember for those who were in a sorority or fraternity.

PNEUMONIA

This word, meaning a disease of the lungs, is often misspelled by dropping or confusing one of the *neu* letters.

You can remember the correct spelling this way: I like to recall that the word is based on the Greek word for breath, spirit, or air, *pneuma*. If this approach is too obscure for you, you might just mispronounce the first part of the word, *pneu*, this way: "pee-nee-you." This technique will give you a device for remembering all of the letters.

PRECEDE

This word, which means to go before or in front of, is most often misspelled "presede" or "preceed."

You can remember the correct spelling this way: It may help to tie this word in with "precedent," which tends to be an easier word to remember.

Also, most words that end with the sound *seed* are spelled *cede*. Only "supersede" is spelled *sede,* and very few—notably "exceed," "succeed," and "proceed"—end in *ceed.*

PREEMINENT

This word, which means outstanding or of the first rank, is most often misspelled by omitting one of the first two *e*'s or by substituting an *e* or an *a* for the *i*.

You can remember the correct spelling first by breaking the word down into two parts: "pre," and "eminent." This division will help you recall there are two *e*'s at the beginning. Also, having the word "eminent" before you makes it easier to remember what is said about that word earlier in this chapter. As you'll see in that entry, "eminent" refers to someone or something that is *e*xcellent.

PREMIER

This word, which means first in importance or position or first in time, is most often misspelled by adding an *e* at the end. (The word "premiere" means a first public performance.)

You can remember the correct spelling this way: That which is premie*r* is fi*r*st ("first" is also a word that has no *e*).

PREMIERE

This word, which means a first public performance, is most often misspelled by dropping the final *e*.

You can remember the correct spelling this way: A pre-mie*re* performance should be a *re*sounding success. Also, you might mispronounce the word by sounding the final *e*.

PRESCRIBE

This word, which means to impose a rule or to write out a medical prescription, is often misspelled by substituting an *o* or an *i* for the first *e*. (The word "proscribe" means to prohibit or condemn as harmful.)

You can remember the correct spelling this way: As you write the word, place a hard, clear emphasis on the first syllable, *pre,* and give the *e* a long sound. Also, it may be helpful to tie in *pre*scribe with *pre*scription, if the latter word is easier for you to remember.

PRESENCE

This word, which means the condition of being present, is often misspelled by substituting an *s* for the *c*.

You can remember the correct spelling this way: One's presen*c*e may be determined by a roll *c*all.

PRINCIPAL

This word may mean the most important; the person who is head of a secondary school; or capital used for investment. It may be confused with "principle," which means a fundamental law or assumption.

You can remember the correct spelling this way: The princip*al* is over *al*l.

PRINCIPLE
This word, which means a fundamental law or assumption, is often misspelled by confusing it with "principal."

You can remember the correct spelling this way: It's *ple*asant to meet a person of princi*ple*.

PRONUNCIATION
This word, which refers to the act of pronouncing something, is often misspelled "pronounciation."

You can remember the correct spelling by noting that the word "pronounce" is *not* included in "pronunciation." Also, you can see that the word "nun" is included.

PROPHECY
This word is the noun that means an utterance in accordance with divine will, or a prediction of the future. It may be incorrectly used in place of the verb "prophesy," which means to predict or to speak with the assurance of divine guidance. The final syllable of "prophecy" is pronounced "see," while the final syllable of "prophesy" is pronounced "sigh." (Note: Although "prophesy" is also acceptable as a noun, the spelling "prophecy" is preferred.)

You can remember the preferred spelling this way: A prophe*c*y is a *c*all to action in the name of God.

PROPHESY
This word is the verb that means to predict or speak with the assurance of divine guidance. It may be incorrectly

spelled like the noun "prophecy," which means an utterance in accordance with divine will, or a prediction of the future.

You can remember the correct spelling this way: To prophe*sy* is to *say* something.

PROSCRIBE
This word, which means to prohibit or condemn as harmful, may be misspelled by substituting an *e* for the *o*. (The word "prescribe" means to give out a medical prescription or to lay down a rule.)

You can remember the correct spelling this way: To *pro*scribe means to *pro*hibit.

RECEIVE
This word, which means to acquire or take possession of something, is often misspelled "recieve."

You can remember the correct spelling this way: This word is an example of the old rule "*i* before *e* except after *c.*"

RECONCILE
This word, which means to bring back harmony or friendship, is often misspelled by substituting an *s* for the second *c.*

You can remember the correct spelling by breaking the word down into three parts: "re," "con," and "cile." Also, use the two *c*'s in the word to remind you that the purpose of re*c*on*c*iliation is to bring *c*onflict to a *c*lose.

RENDEZVOUS

This word, which means a place appointed for a meeting, or the meeting itself, is often misspelled by dropping the *z*.

You can remember the correct spelling this way: As you spell, mispronounce the word to emphasize the *z*. Also, you might think of some absurd association, such as, "The rendezvous of the *z*ebras was the watering hole."

RENOUNCE

This word, which means to resign, refuse, or give up, is often misspelled by substituting a *w* for the *u,* or by substituting an *s* for the *c*.

You can remember the correct spelling by dividing the word into three parts: "re," "no," and "unce." You can remember this last part by noting that it contains most of the letters in *uncle*.

Another possible division, which may be more to your liking, is this: "re," "noun" (this is easy to remember because it's one of the parts of speech), and "ce." This approach can be made more memorable by mispronouncing the three sections: "ree-noun-cee."

RENUNCIATION

This word, which means the act of renouncing or refusing, is often misspelled "renounciation."

You can remember the correct spelling this way: "Renunciation" does *not* contain "renounce." Also, pronouncing the word the right way will help you remember the spelling. Emphasize the "nun" syllable.

REPERTOIRE
This word means a list of things that a person or company is prepared to perform, or a supply of skills. It is often misspelled by dropping the first *r* or by dropping the final *e*.

You can remember the correct spelling by dividing the word into four main parts, all of which are words themselves: "re," "per," "to," and "ire." Also, you might think that a person with a *repertoire* is *re*ady to *per*form, not *to* ret*ire*.

REPERTORY
This word, which means a place where items may be found, or a company that presents a set of plays at a theater, is often misspelled by dropping the first *r* or by inserting an *i* before the last *r*.

You can remember the correct spelling this way: This word contains the smaller words "per" and "tory." Also, pronouncing clearly the *r* in "per" and the last two syllables, "tory," will help.

RESTAURANT
This word, which means a public eating place, is often misspelled by dropping the *au* or by dropping the *u*.

You can remember the correct spelling this way: This word "rest*aura*nt" contains the smaller word "aura."

RESTAURATEUR
This word, which means one who owns or operates a restaurant, may be misspelled in a number of ways: "res-

trateur," "restararateur," "restraunteur," or "restauratuer." The spelling "restauranteur" is acceptable, but "restaurateur" is preferred.

You can remember the preferred spelling this way: "Rest*aura*teur" contains an "aura" but *not* an "ant." Also, the ending "teur" can be remembered by mispronouncing it "tee-ur."

RHYME

This word, which refers to words that have similar sounds, is often misspelled by putting the *y* before the *h* or by inserting an *i*. (The word "rime" is a variant of "rhyme," but "rhyme" is preferred.)

You can remember the correct spelling this way: Because "rhyme" has an unusual and hard-to-remember sequence of letters, it's best to divide it up: "r," "hy," "me." Then you can mispronounce it "rrr-high-me."

RHYTHM

This word, which means a pattern of strong and weak beats in a musical work, may be misspelled by putting the *y* before the *h,* by dropping one of the *h*'s, or by inserting an *i* or other extraneous letters.

You can remember the correct spelling this way: This word has many of the same problems posed by "rhyme." You'll just have to break down the spelling into several parts and memorize each. Here's one possibility: "rhy" and "thm." It will help to note that the letter *h* is the middle letter in each of these parts.

SACCHARIN

This word, which means the extremely sweet substance that is used as a noncaloric sweetener, may be misspelled by adding an *e* at the end or by dropping a *c*. (The word "saccharine" is a descriptive word, or adjective, that means sickishly sweet.)

You can remember the spelling by thinking, "There is a *sack* of *char*coal *in* 'saccharin.' "

SACCHARINE

This word, which means sickishly sweet, is often misspelled by dropping the *e*. (The word "saccharin" means the very sweet substance that is used as a noncaloric sweetener.)

You can remember the correct spelling this way: No real U.S. M*arine* is sacch*arine*.

SALMON

This word, which means a type of game fish, is often misspelled by dropping or misplacing the *l*.

You can remember the correct spelling this way: Mispronounce the word by emphasizing the *l*.

SANDWICH

This word, which means at least one slice of bread covered with an edible filling, is often misspelled by dropping the *d*.

You can remember the correct spelling by emphasizing the *d* as you pronounce.

SAPPHIRE

This word, which means a colorful gem, is often mis-spelled by dropping a *p,* including an *f* in place of the *ph,* or dropping or misplacing the *e.*

You can remember the correct spelling this way: Divide the word into three parts, and mispronounce accordingly: "sap," "phi," and "re."

Your mispronunciation would be "sap-phy-ree."

SAXOPHONE

This word, which refers to the curved woodwind instru-ment, is often misspelled by substituting an *a* for the first *o.*

You can remember the correct spelling this way: As you prepare to spell, emphasize the *o* in your pronunciation.

SCALPEL

This word, which means the small knife used in surgery, is often misspelled by dropping the first *l.*

You can remember the correct spelling this way: First you should note that the word "scalp" is present in "*scal-p*el." Also, you might mispronounce by emphasizing the first *l.*

SEIZE

This word, which means to take possession of something, is often misspelled by putting the *i* before the first *e,* or by substituting an *s* for the *z.*

You can remember the correct spelling by dividing the word into three parts: "se," "i," and "ze." You'll note that the first and last parts end in an *e*. It should help to mispronounce this "see-eye-zee."

Note: The standard rule "*i* before *e* except after *c*" does *not* apply here. In other words, "seize" is an exception to the rule.

SEPARATE

This word, which means set apart, or not shared with another, is often misspelled by substituting an *e* for the first *a*.

You can remember the correct spelling this way: Mispronounce by emphasizing the *a*.

SEWAGE

This word, which means waste materials carried off in sewers, is often misspelled by inserting *er* after the *w*. (The word "sewerage" means the process of removing sewage, or the system of pipes and other structures that carry off sewage.)

You can remember the correct spelling this way: The word "sewage" doesn't contain a "sewer." Also, it may help to divide the word into the two shorter words "sew" and "age."

SEWER

This word may mean a manmade underground pipe that carries off sewage (pronounced "suh-wer"), or a person who sews with needle and thread (pronounced "soh-wer"). The word used with the first meaning isn't often misspelled; but the word used with the second meaning is frequently misspelled "sower." (The word "sower" means one who plants seed.)

You can remember the correct spelling of "sewer," meaning one who sews with needle and thread, this way: A *seamstress* is a *sewer*.

SEWERAGE

This word means the process of removing sewage, or the system of pipes and other structures that carry off sewage. Its spelling is often confused with that of "sewage," which means the waste material carried off in a sewerage system.

You can remember the correct spelling this way: Pronounce the word correctly, with three syllables, and you'll spell it correctly.

SHENANIGAN

This word, which means a devious trick or other questionable conduct, is often misspelled by doubling one of the letters.

You can remember the correct spelling this way: The word contains no double letters.

SHERBET, SHERBERT

There is some confusion in various dictionaries about this word, which means a cold drink consisting of a fruit juice mixture, or an ice dessert consisting of milk, egg whites, or gelatin. According to some authorities, the first spelling for any of the definitions should be "sherbet," with "sherbert" sometimes listed as an alternative. Other authorities say that the spelling should be "sherbet" when a drink is intended, and "sherbert" should be used for the more solid, ice dessert.

My inclination is to use "sherbet" for all cases—unless you're in the mood to explain why you've used "sherbert." But if you prefer the sherbet-sherbert distinction described above, you'll find authority for it in *Webster's Ninth New Collegiate Dictionary,* published by Merriam-Webster.

You can remember the correct spellings this way: With the "bet" version, think you're *bet*ting on a tasty treat. With the "bert" version, think "Herbert."

SILHOUETTE
This word, which means the outline of a shape which is dark and featureless, is often misspelled by dropping the *h* or the *u,* or omitting a *t.*

You can remember the correct spelling this way: Mispronounce by emphasizing the *h,* the *u,* and the *te.* For example, you might say, "sil-hoo-you-et-tee."

SITE
This word, which means a scene, location, or designated spot where a structure is to be built, is often misspelled by substituting a *c* for the *s.* (The word "cite" means to call upon or quote an authority.)

You can remember the correct spelling this way: "Site" should remind you of a *s*cene or a *s*tructure.

SMORGASBORD
This word, which means a buffet offering a mixture of foods and snacks, may be misspelled in a number of ways,

including the following: "smorgusbord," "smorgasboard," and "smorgisbord."

You can remember the correct spelling this way: Think in terms of these words, which echo the syllables and letters of the word: "*some more*," "*gas*," and "*bored.*"

SOPHOMORE

This word, which means a second-year student in a secondary school or college, is commonly misspelled "sophmore" or "sothmore."

You can remember the correct spelling this way: Pronounce the word correctly, so that the *ph* sounds like an *f*, not a *t*. Then mispronounce to emphasize the middle *o*, which is silent in proper pronunciation.

SOWER

This word, which means one who plants seed, is often misspelled by confusing it with "sewer," which means to sew with a needle and thread.

You can remember the correct spelling this way: A *sow*er may plant food to feed a *sow*.

SPAGHETTI

This word, which refers to the stringlike version of pasta, is often misspelled by dropping the *g* or the *h*.

You can remember the correct spelling this way: Mispronounce the word as "spag-hetti," with an emphasis on the *g* and the *h*.

SPECTER

This word, which means a ghost, may be spelled "spectre," though "specter" is preferred.

You can remember the preferred spelling this way: A spec*ter* may cause *terr*or.

STANCH
This word, which means to stop the flow of something, such as blood, is often misspelled by inserting a *u* before the *n*. (The word "staunch" means strongly built. Note: The spelling "staunch" is a variant of "stanch," but "stanch" is better when the meaning is to stop the flow of something.)

You can remember the correct spelling this way: When you "*stan*ch," you want to make the flowing liquid *stan*d still.

STATIONARY
This word, which means immobile or in a fixed position, is often misspelled by substituting an *e* for the second *a*. (The word "stationery" means materials used for writing or typing.)

You can remember the correct spelling this way: That which is statio*nary* is *n*ow *a*t *r*est.

STATIONERY
This word, which refers to the materials used for writing or typing, is often misspelled by substituting an *a* for the *e*. (The word "stationary" means immobile or in a fixed position.)

You can remember the correct spelling this way: Station*ery* is used by a writ*er*.

STAUNCH

This word, which means strongly built, is often misspelled by dropping the *u*. (The word "stanch" means to stop the flow of something. Note: The spelling "stanch" is a variation of "staunch," but when the meaning is strongly built, "staunch" is preferred.)

You can remember the correct spelling this way: A st*aunch* platform is necessary for a rocket l*aunch*.

SUBTLE

This word, which means hard to comprehend or characterized by unusual insight or craftiness, is often misspelled by dropping the *b* or by using an incorrect ending, such as *tel* or *til*.

You can remember the correct spelling this way: The word "subtle" contains all the letters of "sublet" in order—except that the *t* is out of order.

SUCCESSFUL

This word, which means being in a state of success or achievement, is often misspelled by dropping a *c* or an *s*, or by adding an *l* at the end.

You can remember the correct spelling by dividing it into three parts: "suc," "cess," and "ful." Also, memorize the fact that there are two *c*'s and *s*'s, but only one *l*.

SUMMARY

This word, which means a shorter version containing the main points of a longer presentation, is often misspelled by substituting an *e* for the *a*. (The word "summery" means relating to or reminiscent of summer.)

You can remember the correct spelling this way: The *sum* of *Mary*'s lambs was one.

SUMMERY

This word, which means relating to or reminiscent of summer, is often misspelled by substituting an *a* for the *e*. (The word "summary" means a shorter version containing the main points of a longer presentation.)

You can remember the correct spelling this way: The word "summer" is contained in "*summery*."

SUPERSEDE

This word, which means to take the place of or to cause to be put aside, is often spelled "supercede." Both spellings are correct, but the first, "supersede," is preferred.

You can remember the preferred spelling this way: That which super*sede*s *s*hoves something else aside.

SUSCEPTIBLE

This word, which means open to being influenced, may be misspelled in several ways: "suseptible," "suceptible," "susceptable," or "suseptable."

You can remember the correct spelling by breaking the word down into three parts: "sus," "cep," and "tible." Note that a *c* follows the second *s* and also that there is no "table" (only a "tible") in this word.

SYNONYMOUS

This word, which means being alike in significance or meaning, is often misspelled by dropping one or both *y*'s or by substituting an *i* for a *y*. Also, the ending may be misspelled *mos* or *mus*.

You can remember the correct spelling by breaking the word down into its component parts: "sy-no-ny-mous." Also, mispronounce to emphasize each *y* and the *mous* ending (you might mispronounce the ending "mouse").

THEIR

This word, which means belonging to them, is often misspelled "there." (The word "there" means at a certain place.)

You can remember the correct spelling this way: "T*heir* contains the word "*heir*."

THERE

This word, which means at a certain place, is often misspelled "their." (The word "their" means belonging to them.)

You can remember the correct spelling this way: "T*here*" contains a related word, "*here.*"

THEY'RE

This word, which is the contraction for "they are," is often misspelled "there." (The word "there" means at a certain place.)

You can remember the correct spelling this way: The apostrophe indicates that letters are missing; hence, "they're" is a contraction.

THRESHOLD
This word, which means the hard surface that lies at the base of a door, is often misspelled by adding an extra *h* or an extra *s*.

You can remember the correct spelling this way: This word contains the two smaller words "thresh" and "old." Also, just memorize the fact that there are no double letters.

TORT
This word, which means a wrongful act that may trigger a civil lawsuit, is often misspelled by adding an *e*. (The word "torte" means a cakelike pastry cooked with eggs and covered with a frosting.)

You can remember the correct spelling this way: A tort may spark a legal re*tort*.

TORTE
This word, which means a cakelike pastry cooked with eggs and covered with a frosting, is often misspelled by dropping the final *e*.

You can remember the correct spelling this way: A tort*e* is for d*e*ss*e*rt.

TORTUOUS
This word, which means winding or twisting, is often misspelled by inserting an *r* after the *u*. Also, the ending may be incorrectly spelled by omitting the *o* or one of the *u*'s. (The word "torturous" means relating to or causing torture.)

You can remember the correct spelling this way: Pronounce to emphasize the *u* and omit any second *r* sound. The ending should be mispronounced to emphasize the *ous*.

TORTUROUS

This word, which means hurting, painful, or relating to or causing torture, is often misspelled by omitting the second *r*. (The word "tortuous" means winding or twisting.)

You can remember the correct spelling this way: Most of "*torture*" is contained in "*torture*ous."

TWELFTH

This word, which refers to a person, day, or other item that is number twelve in order, is often misspelled "twelfh," "twelvth," "twelveth," or "twelvefth."

You can remember the correct spelling this way: Pronounce the word correctly to get the *f* and *th* sounds. Then think, "This word *doesn't* contain the *ve* in 'twelve.' "

UNNECESSARY

This word, which means not necessary, is often misspelled by dropping an *n*, adding a *c*, or dropping an *s*.

You can remember the correct spelling by breaking the word down into two parts: "un" and "necessary." Perhaps just seeing the word "necessary" will help you remember the correct spelling. If not, mispronounce it "nee-cee-sa-ree." Note that there are two doubled letters, *n* and *s*, but no doubled *c*.

VACCINATE
This word, which means injecting dead microorganisms into the body to produce immunity and prevent a disease (especially the use of a cowpox vaccine to prevent smallpox), is often misspelled by dropping a *c* or adding an *n.*

You can remember the correct spelling by breaking the word down into three parts: "vac," "cin," and "ate." Also, note that much of "*acci*dent" is contained in "v*acci*nate."

VACILLATE
This word, which means to waver, is often misspelled by adding an *s,* by dropping the *c,* or by dropping an *l.*

You can remember the correct spelling by thinking in terms of these three parts of the word, two of which are smaller words: "vac," "ill," and "ate."

VAGUE
This word, which means indefinite or unclearly expressed, is often misspelled by dropping the *u* or placing it before the *g.*

You can remember the correct spelling by mispronouncing with two syllables: "vag-you."

VAIN
This word, which means without value or showing excessive pride, is often misspelled "vane." (The word "vane" means a device that moves about to indicate the direction of the wind.)

You can remember the correct spelling this way: Va*i*n

contains an *I*, which should remind you that a vain person is egotistically "I-oriented."

VANE
This word, which means a device that moves about to indicate the direction of the wind, is often misspelled "vain." (The word "vain" means without value, or showing excessive pride.)

You can remember the correct spelling this way: If the force of the wind *wanes*, a weather *vane* may not be necessary.

VEGETABLE
This word, which refers to a large group of edible plants, is often misspelled by dropping the second *e*, by substituting an *a* for the second *e*, or by substituting an *i* for the *a*.

You can remember the correct spelling by breaking the word down in one or more ways. One possibility is "vege-table." Here, you have the word "'table" and a clear emphasis on the correct letters in *vege.*

Another possibility is "ve-get-able." Here, you have the words "get" and "able." You'll have to memorize the first two letters, *ve.*

VEIL
This word, which means something that hides something else, such as a cloth covering for the face, is often misspelled "vail" or "vale." (The word "vail" means to lower, while "vale" means a valley.)

You can remember the correct spelling this way: The two most difficult letters in the word "ve*i*l" are contained in the word "h*id*e," and a veil is used to hide something. (But note that the *e* comes before the *i* in "veil," as an exception to the *i* before *e* rule.)

WAIVER

This word, which means the abandoning of a right, may be misspelled "waver." (The word "waver" means to fluctuate or move unsteadily.)

You can remember the correct spelling by thinking, "This word has an *i,* which reminds me of 'r*i*ghts.'"

WAVER

This word, which means to fluctuate or move unsteadily, is often misspelled "waiver." (The word "waiver" means the abandoning of a right.)

You can remember the correct spelling this way: That which *wave*rs may *wave* back and forth.

WEATHER

This word, which means atmospheric conditions, including rain, wind, or snow, is often misspelled "whether." (The word "whether" is a linking word—known as a conjunction—that is used to indicate an indirect question, or a choice between two things or situations.)

You can remember the correct spelling this way: If the w*eat*her is nice, you can *eat* outdoors.

WHETHER

This word is a linking word (a conjunction) that is used to indicate an indirect question, or a choice between two things or situations. It is often misspelled "weather." (The word "weather" means atmospheric conditions, including rain, wind, or snow.)

You can remember the correct spelling this way: "Whether" contains two complete smaller words, "whet" and "her."

YOUR
This word, which indicates ownership or possession by "you," is often misspelled "you're." ("You're" is a contraction of "you are.")

You can remember the correct spelling this way: Note that no apostrophe is used to show that "you" has ownership.

YOU'RE
This word, which is the contraction for "you are," is often misspelled "your." (The word "your" indicates ownership or possession by "you.")

You can remember the correct spelling this way: The presence of an apostrophe between two sets of letters should remind you that a letter has been left out—and so a contraction is involved.

These words, which are in common use in everyday and business communication, are the ones that I find to be the toughest to spell. You should feel free to add your own pet problem words to this "toughest" list. That way, you'll tailor the list to your own needs—and you'll find your spelling ability increasing even more.

Is it possible to generalize about the spelling techniques suggested in this list? There are some helpful rules that apply when you encounter a difficult word—though as we'll see in the next chapter, a number of caveats and qualifications have to be kept in mind with any rule of spelling.

3
Rules with Some Rhyme and Reason

The English language—including the subspecialty of spelling—is loaded with rules. But for every rule, there is almost always at least one exception. The various conditions and qualifications make English spelling a particularly difficult task. Consequently, those aspiring to rise above the Terrible Speller category may be tempted to disregard the rules entirely.

My suggestion to you: Don't succumb to this temptation! The rules may have their limitations, but at least they afford some guidance and provide a starting point for improvement of spelling.

In this chapter, I want to remind you of some rules you probably already know and also introduce you to a few that you may not have encountered. In later chapters, we'll explore other rules that relate to special topics, like the beginnings and endings of words.

Rule 1: i before e
Almost everyone who has completed elementary school knows this old rhyme:

> *Put i before e except after c,*
> *Or when the sound is long a as in "neighbor" or*
> *"weigh."*

Unfortunately, even though the above rhyme states an accurate rule for many words, there are also a large number of exceptions. For example, the words "weird," "foreign," "leisure," and "financier" don't follow the rule.

So how can you use the rule and avoid most of the pitfalls that occur when an exception pops up? There are a number of explanations, some of them rather complex or detailed, that can deal with the majority of the exceptions. One of these corollaries is that in most cases, when the *c* sounds like *sh,* the order of the letters is *ie,* not *ei.* (Examples are "ancient" and "efficient.")

But most people don't have time or inclination to memorize and learn to apply such detailed guidelines. Instead, I'd recommend you use this approach:

First, memorize the basic rule if you haven't already done so. The simple rhyme will help you spell many tough words like "receive" (note the *c*); "sleigh" (note the *a* sound); "wield" (*i* before *e*); and "grieve" (*i* before *e*).

Second, think of *ie* and *ei* words that give you particular trouble. "Weird" is one of the words that has always frustrated me. "Foreign" gives other people trouble. "Financier" can be a particular bugaboo, even for those working on Wall Street!

When you've catalogued your most troublesome *ie* and *ei* words, just add an extra few words or a line to the rhyme:

> *Put i before e except after c*
> *(but not in "financier"),*
> *Or when the sound is long a as in*
> *"neighbor" or "weigh"—*
> *And don't forget "foreign" and "weird."*

This approach may do violence to the rhyme. But it will help you remember the words that pose the greatest threat to accuracy. You don't have to learn every exception, of course—only those unusual *ei* or *ie* words that frequently trigger your spelling errors.

Rule 2: u after q

This rule is about as absolute and free of exceptions as any you'll find: Always put *u* after *q*.

This short precept will help you remember such words as "quarter," "quantity," "equality," and "question."

There are very few exceptions, and for the most part they involve words of foreign origin, many of which are not the most common spellings in use. An illustration is "qabbala," a variant of the more common "cabala," the system of mystical Jewish philosophy.

There are also *q*'s without a following *u* that are used in abbreviations. One of these is "qt" or "QT," an abbreviation for "quiet," as in, "keep this on the qt." Another is "mind your *p*'s and *q*'s." (This phrase, which means to be careful, may be rooted in the admonition to children to watch carefully the subtle distinction between the letter *p* and the letter *q* when they are learning handwriting.)

For ordinary words, however—excluding the few exceptions involving foreign words and abbreviations—the *u* after *q* rule holds.

Rule 3: No loss of letters or syllables

I've already mentioned the importance of proper pronunciation in earlier sections of this book. We've seen that *mis*-pronunciation may sometimes help you to remember the spelling of a word. This technique may work, for instance, when you sound the *e* in "noticeable" (no-ti-*cee*-able).

A knowledge of good pronunciation is even more important than the strategic use of mispronunciation. It's true that the English language has a number of words, like "rhyme" and "reason," which are spelled differently from the way they sound. Despite these limitations, knowing the correct pronunciation can frequently eliminate many spelling errors. Here are some words that commonly lose a letter or syllable, often as a result of defective pronunciation. In those cases where good pronunciation doesn't help, you'll have to fall back on one of the memorization techniques discussed in the previous chapter.

ACCIDENTALLY. The word may be mispronounced with only four syllables as "accidently." Correctly using all five syllables will help you keep the *al*.

ACCOMPANIMENT. The second *a* or another letter may be dropped because of dropping a syllable in pronunciation. Or a *y* may be substituted for the *i*. To remember the *i*, think, "The word '*anim*al' is mostly present in 'accomp*anim*ent.' "

ACREAGE. It's best to give a slight sound to the *e* when you pronounce this word. Otherwise, you may end up with "acrage" or, if the *e* is there but misplaced, "acerage."

ANECDOTE. A common mistaken variation is "antidote," which results from the wrong pronunciation. (Of course, "antidote" is a legitimate word, but it often is substituted when the writer or speaker means "anecdote.")

ASKED. Because some people mispronounce this word "ast" or some other way, they may use bizarre spellings such as "askd," "askt," "ackst," "axst," or the like.

ASTERISK. Mispronunciations may cause this one to come out "aterisk," "askterisk," or "acksterisk."

BROCCOLI. It's easy to drop a *c* or add an *l* with this common vegetable. (Some dictionaries say that "brocoli" is an acceptable variation, but others don't include it; it's best to stick with "broccoli.") The correct pronunciation won't help you here, but you might remember the spelling by dividing the word into two parts: "broccoli."

CALISTHENICS. This very commonly misspelled word can become one of your easy-to-spell words if you stress slightly the sounds of the first *i* and the *e*. Otherwise, you'll end up with "calesthenics" or "calesthinics."

CATEGORY. Just a slight, subtle shift in pronunciation may change the *e* to an *a*, with the erroneous "catagory" being the result.

CEMETERY. Emphasizing the third *e* as an *a* may cause the misspelling "cemetary."

CHARACTERISTIC. A frequent mistake is to neglect to pronounce all five syllables correctly. If you slip into this trap, you may spell the word "charactristic," "charcter-istic," or "charateristic."

CHOCOLATE. Again, the second *o* may be dropped in speech, with the resulting error "choclate."

DISASSEMBLE. Dropping the *as* when you talk will result in "dissemble," which is a word, but not the right word.

ENVIRONMENT. The second *n* is frequently omitted in speech to give you "envirment" or "enviroment" in spelling. Sometimes just the *o* is omitted, producing "envirnment."

GENEALOGY. Good pronunciation doesn't help here because one of the most common mistakes with this word is to drop the *a* and substitute an *o*. An effective way to remember this frequently lost letter is to think "*a*ncestor."

GOVERNMENT. A *very* common mistake is to leave out the *n* in pronunciation and to misspell the word "goverment."

GRAMMAR. Making the last *a* sound too much like an *e* may result in "grammer."

INCIDENTALLY. There are *five* syllables in this word. Many times, the *al* is dropped and the word incorrectly spelled "incidently."

LABORATORY. Often, the *o* may be omitted in pronunciation to produce the erroneous "labratory" or "labrotory."

LIBRARY. If the first *r* isn't pronounced, you may end up with "libary" or "liberry."

OUTRAGEOUS. The mistake here may be to drop the *e* or change it to an *i*. Because the pronunciation doesn't identify the *e,* you may have to mispronounce with a long *e* as a memory device. So you might say, "out-rag-eee-ous."

PLAINTIFF. The *t* is sometimes dropped, making "plainiff," because in improper pronunciation, the *t* isn't sounded. Also, an *f* may be omitted. You might think that a plain-*tiff* is one who starts a "tiff," or quarrel, in court.

QUANTITY. A similar mistake occurs when the first *t* is dropped here, with "quanity" being the result.

REPRESENTATIVE. Many people drop the first *t* when they're talking, and this mistake may cause them to spell the word "represenative."

SACRILEGIOUS. This well-known word isn't used too much in business or personal writing. But when the occasion arises to employ it, a frequent error is to spell it "sac-riligious" or "sacreligious."

SEPARATE. This tough word is easier to spell as a verb than an adjective because with the verb form, the first *a* comes across more clearly. Otherwise, you misspell it "seperate."

TEMPERAMENT. *Correct* pronunciation can lead you into a mistake here and cause you to misspell this word "tem-prament," or "temprement," or "temperment." So you might use a variant pronunciation that allows the sounding of two syllables with the *pera* letters.

TEMPERATURE. It's common in everyday speech to drop the *a* and use only three syllables, but if you fall into this habit, you could misspell the word "temperture." So be sure to use all four syllables.

TREACHEROUS. Correct pronunciation leaves out the *a,* and so you'll have to resort to other means to remember, such as mispronouncing to highlight the *a*. This way you'll avoid "trecherous."

VALUABLE. The second *a* can be lost unless you place at least a slight emphasis on it in spelling. Otherwise, you'll err with "valuble" or some variation.

WEDNESDAY. Correct pronunciation won't help you here. So you may find it helpful to mispronounce to help you remember the *dnes*. Otherwise, you may misspell it "Wendsday" or "Wensday."

Now, add your own troublesome words to this list, and continue adding as you think of additional ones in the future.

Rule 4: No adding extra letters or syllables
As with the previous rule, mispronunciation can be a major culprit in this mistake. Here are some common boo-boos:

ATHLETE. A frequent mispronunciation is to add an extra sound, "athalete" or "athelete."

DISASTROUS. It's understandable, but incorrect, to include "disaster" in this word. So say it properly and stay away from "disasterous."

GRIEVOUS. Another frequent blunder is to insert an *e* sound after the *v* to make it "grieveous" or "grievious."

HINDRANCE. Here, it's tempting to include "hinder," but that will give you "hinderance," which is wrong.

LIGHTNING. The bolt of electricity in the sky on a stormy night is "lightning," *not* "lightening" (adding the *e* indicates you want to say that something is getting less dark). Being careful with your pronunciation will help you keep out the extra syllable and letter.

MISCHIEVOUS. There may even be a majority of people who mispronounce this word "mischievious" and also misspell it that way (or "mischieveous"). Stay away from the extra sound of *i.*

PERSEVERANCE. Perhaps the most common mistake with this word is to add an *r* after *perse.* Correct pronunciation will help you keep this unwanted *r* out.

TENET. This word, which means a belief or principle often held in common by a group or organization, may be misspelled by adding an *n* or an *a.* For example: "tenent," "tennet," or "tenant." ("Tenant" means a renter, or one who occupies the property of another.) Correct pronunciation should help you keep the *a* and the extra *n* out.

As before, add your own special tough words, and continue to build up your list as you write and talk.

Rule 5: k after a hard c ending

With some words that end in *c,* the final sound is described as "hard," like a *k.* Adding certain extra letters and syllables after the final *c*—such as *i, y,* or *e*—may tend to turn the hard sound into a soft *s* sound. In such situations, a *k* will be added after the final *c.* Here are some illustrations:

MIMICKED, MIMICKING, MIMICKER. These verb and noun forms of the verb "mimic" can be tricky, not only because of the *k* ending, but also because there are two *m*'s and two *i*'s.

PANICKED, PANICKING, PANICKY. These words, which include some of the verb and adjective forms of "panic," are pronounced with a *k* sound at the end and spelled the same way.

PICNICKED, PICNICKING, PICNICKER. The same rule applies here with these verb and noun forms of "picnic." But don't become confused and add an extra *k,* as in "picnicking."

POLITICK, POLITICKING. With this word, which is the verb meaning to engage in politics, you have to be aggressive and confident in sounding that *k*. Those who are unsure of themselves will drop the *k* in spelling, often because "it just doesn't look right"—and they'll be dead wrong!

Note: Unlike many of the other words ending in a hard *c,* the present tense of this verb is "politick," not "politic."

TRAFFICKED, TRAFFICKING, TRAFFICKER. This is a verb form of "traffic." Also, don't forget the double *f.*

Rule 6: No scrambling letters

Sometimes, because of mispronunciation, carelessness, or simple ignorance, a writer may use the right letters, but in the wrong order. The result can be a mixup or scrambling of letters that may actually make the word hard to decipher.

In most cases, being careful and attending to correct pronunciation can help you avoid these errors. Also, it helps to have in mind a "most-mixed-up" list, including particular words that give you scrambling problems. Here are some of the most frequent mixed-letter mistakes that I've encountered. In some cases, I've followed up the "common scrambling" illustrations with other frequent spelling errors. Look them over and then add some of your own.

AESTHETIC. Common scrambling: "aeshtetic" or "estheatic."

ALLEGIANCE. Common scrambling: "alligeance," "alleigance," or "allegaince."

ANALYSIS. Common scrambling: "analsyis."

ANALYZE. Common scrambling: "anylaze" or "analzye."

ANONYMOUS. Common scrambling: "anyonmous." Another possible mistake is "anonimous."

ANTECEDENT Common scrambling: "anteceednt." Also, the word may be misspelled "anticedent," "antecident," or "antecedant."

AUXILIARY. Common scrambling: "auxilairy."

BUREAUCRACY. Common scrambling: "buraceuracy" or "bureacuracy."

CALISTHENICS. Common scrambling: "calesthinics." Also, a common misspelling is "calesthenics."

CONSCIENTIOUS. Common scrambling: "contienscious," "consceintious."

DIAPHRAGM. Common scrambling: "diagphram," "diapraghm," or "diaphrgam."

ENTREPRENEUR. Common scrambling: "enterpreneur," "entreperneur," or "entreprenuer."

GASOLINE. Common scrambling: "gasolien." An even more common mistake is to spell it "gasolene."

GAUGE. Common scrambling: "guage" or "gague."

GORGEOUS. Common scrambling: "gorgoeus." Also, the *e* may be omitted mistakenly.

HARANGUE. Common scrambling: "haraunge" or "haragnue."

HEIGHT. Common scrambling: "hieght," "heigth," or "hiegth."

HEINOUS. Common scrambling: "hienous." Also, the *i* may be erroneously dropped.

HEMORRHAGE. Common scrambling: "hemorrahge," "hemohrrage," or "hemorhrage." Also, an extra *m* may be added, or an *r* or the second *h* may be dropped.

HEMORRHOID. Common scrambling: "hemohrroid," "hemorhroid," or "hemorrohid." Also, an *m* may be added, or an *r* or the second *h* may be omitted.

HIERARCHY. Common scrambling: "heirarchy."

HORS D'OEUVRE. Common scrambling: "hors d'oeurve," "hors d'ouevre," or "hors d'oeuver."

IRRELEVANT. Very common scrambling: "irrevelant." Also, "irrelavent."

KHAKI. Common scrambling: "kahki" or "kakhi."

LANGUOROUS. Common scrambling: "langourous" or "languoruos."

LINGERIE. Common scrambling: "lingiree" or "lengirie."

MILEAGE. Common scrambling: "milaege." Also, the *a* may be omitted erroneously.

OBSEQUIOUS. Common scrambling: "obsiqueous."

PARADIGM. Common scrambling: "paradimg," "paridagm," or "paragdim." Also, the word may be misspelled "paradime."

PERSPIRATION. Common scrambling: "prespiration" or "pirsperation."

PERVERSE. Common scrambling: "preverse."

PHARAOH. Common scrambling: "pharoah" or "phaorah." Also, a frequent mistake is "pharoh."

PHYSIOLOGIC. Common scrambling: "psyhiologic" or "phisyologic."

POEM. Common scrambling: "pome" or "peom."

PSYCHOLOGY. Common scrambling: "pyschology," "psyhcology," or "psycohlogy."

RECONNAISSANCE. Common scrambling: "reconaissannce." Also, an extra *c* may be added, or a *c* or *s* may be dropped.

RESUSCITATE. Common scrambling: "resucsitate" or "recussitate." Also, the second *s* or the *c* may be dropped.

RHAPSODY. Common scrambling: "raphsody" or "rapsodhy." Also, the *h* may be omitted.

RHYME. Common scrambling: "ryhme" or "rhyem."

RHYTHM. Common scrambling: "ryhthm" or "rthyhm."

SAPPHIRE. Common scrambling: "saphpire" or "sapphier." Also, a *p* or the *h* may be dropped.

SERGEANT. Common scrambling: "seargent." Also, the word may be misspelled "sargent" or "sargeant."

SYRINGE. Common scrambling: "syrnige" or "syirnge."

TRAGEDY. Common scrambling: "tradegy." Also, the word may often be misspelled "tradgedy."

UNCONSCIONABLE. Common scrambling: "unconcsionable" or "unconsioncable."

WEIGHT. Common scrambling: "wieght" or "weiguth."

YIELD. Common scrambling: "yeild."

These six rules will get you started thinking systematically about spelling. As I've said, none of them is ironclad. Each—even the *u* after *q* rule—has some exceptions. But they are all useful as a starting point. Now, let's take a brief breather from rules and consider a few simple principles of Latin.

4
Latin in 20 Minutes— and Other Incredible Foreign Language Feats

Many English words have Latin roots. For example, the Latin verb *amo,* which means "I love," is the basis for English words like "amorous." So if you know Latin, you're several steps ahead in understanding the spelling and definition of many English words.

But what if you've never taken Latin? To learn Latin typically requires at least one year for the basic grammar and then a couple of additional years to build vocabulary and gain facility in reading and translation.

You don't need that kind of intense study to make use of some of the basics of Latin. In fact, you only need about twenty minutes—the time it will take you to read this chapter and think a little about the information and principles contained in it. And to emphasize further how little time and work are required, I'm also going to include some tips on the spelling of other foreign words that are part of common English usage.

A Little Lesson in Using Latin in Your Spelling

A strategic knowledge of some points of Latin grammar and Latin words can be extremely helpful in enhancing your spelling.

But let me begin this little lesson with a warning: Assuming you know too much Latin can be dangerous to your spelling unless you really are an expert. If you stick closely to the points I'm about to make, you'll probably find your English spelling will grow stronger. But don't stray too far from these simple principles or you may find that a little Latin is worse than none at all.

One of the main advantages of learning a little Latin is that it can provide you with an additional memory device. You've probably noted that Latin roots are often listed in the dictionary. If you have trouble remembering the spelling of a particular word and if it has a Latin root, use that information to help you remember the English. Thinking of the foreign roots of words can be a stimulating experience *and* can serve as quite a useful mnemonic device for correct spelling.

For example, if you know that the Latin word for "I love" is *amo,* you're more likely to get the spelling of "*amo*rous" right and not fall into the trap of spelling it "amerous" or "amurous." Similarly, if you know that the word for a female friend is *amica,* you'll probably spell "*amica*ble" correctly.

So that you'll be able to deal more effectively with your dictionary and with the key Latin vocabulary words that will be listed later, let me introduce you at this point to some basics of Latin grammar. You don't have to memorize any of this unless you particularly want to. The main idea at this point is just to get a "feel" for the language.

Latin action words

Latin action words, or verbs, are expressed in a different way from verbs in English. In English, the person acting is expressed as a separate word, usually positioned before the verb. For example, we say, "*I* love." In Latin, however, the personal pronoun "I" is indicated by the ending *o*, as in *amo*.

Similarly, other special endings on verbs are used to express other personal pronouns, such as "you," "he, she, it," "we," and "they." Here are the different endings of *amo*, which indicate the shift to different persons and personal pronouns. I've italicized the special endings that signal the change in pronouns.

am*o*—I love   am*amus*—we love
am*as*—you (singular) love   am*atis*—you (plural) love
am*at*—he, she, it loves   am*ant*—they love

The infinitive of *amo*, by the way—which is translated "to love"—is *amare*.

There are many other types of verb forms, such as those with infinitives that end in *ire* or *ere*. A detailed discussion of these is beyond our present purposes. But occasionally, when I refer to different verb forms in later discussions of words that have Latin roots, you may find it helpful at least to be aware of some of these basics of how Latin verbs differ from those in English.

Latin naming words

Latin naming words, or nouns, frequently serve as the basis for certain important English words. An illustration is the Latin word for son, *filius,* from which we get our word "filial," meaning relating to a son or daughter. In this case, you can see that if you remember the root *filius,* you'll be likely to spell "filial" with an *f* instead of a *ph* and with a second *i* instead of a mistaken *e.* (Common spelling mistakes with this word are "philial" and "fileal.")

Another example is the English word "puerile," which means childish. This comes from the Latin *puer,* meaning boy or child. With the Latin root in mind, you'll be more likely to get the spelling right. Without the Latin, you might fall into the common fallacy "peurile."

As with verbs, there are many different noun endings in the Latin, and only a classical scholar will have many of them at his fingertips as he spells. For your English spelling, you really only need to know these three types of endings, which indicate the singular and plural of Latin words.

- *Ending 1:* The singular of some Latin words is indicated by a *um* ending; the plural of these is formed by changing the ending to *a.* (Example: "datum," "data.")
- *Ending 2:* The singular of other Latin words is indicated by an *a* ending; the plural of these is formed by

switching to an *ae* ending. (Example: "alumna," "alumnae.")

- *Ending 3:* Finally, the singular of other Latin words is indicated by a *us* ending; the plural of these words is made by switching to a final *i*. (Example: "alumnus," "alumni.")

Other Latin words

Various adjectives, adverbs, prepositions, and other words in Latin also pop up periodically in English. Here are a few that are encountered frequently:

MAGNA. This word, which means great or large, is the basis for many English words, including "magnate." A common misspelling of "magnate" is "magnet," but you'd never make that mistake if you knew the root.

ANTIQUA. This Latin word means old or ancient, and is the root for "antiquated." The English word may be misspelled "antequated" by those who don't recall the Latin.

SINE. This Latin preposition, which means without, can be found in some words in common use in English. One is "sinecure," which is from the Latin *sine cura,* "without cure of souls." A "sinecure" is a position that requires little or no work but provides compensation. If you don't know the Latin base, it's easy to spell this "sinicure." A purely Latin phrase that is often heard and seen in English is "sine qua non," which means literally "without which not" and indicates an essential item or point.

PAUCI. This Latin adjective means few. The root can be

found in English words like "paucity," meaning a scarcity.

There are also a number of Latin prepositions and prefixes that appear with some regularity in English words. Some of these words can be used in Latin as independent prepositions, or may also be used as prefixes (such as *ad*). Others (such as *dis*) must always be joined to another word as a prefix.

These prepositions and prefixes may occur in English exactly as they are spelled in the Latin, or one or more of the later letters may be changed (the first letter almost always stays the same). Here are some of the most common Latin prepositions and prefixes that you'll see in English.

AB. from, by. Examples: *ab*stain, *ab*sence.

AD. to. Examples: *an*nihilate, *ad*vertising.

ANTE. before. Examples: *ante*bellum, *ante*cedent.

CIRCUM. around. Examples: *circum*vent, *circum*scribe.

CONTRA. against. Examples: *Counter*productive, *contra*diction.

CUM (COM). with, greatly. Examples: *com*poser, *com*pletely, *col*laborator (one who works with), *con*nect.

DE. from, down, out of. Examples: *de*votion, *de*pression, *de*toxification.

DIS. not, apart. Examples: *dif*ference, *dis*tinguished, *dis*approve.

EX. from, out of. Examples: *ex*it, *ef*ficient, *ex*ceed.

IN. into, in, on. Also, may mean "not" or "without." Examples: *in*novative, *ir*regular.

INTER. among, between. Examples: *inter*rupt, *inter*loper.

INTRO. within. Examples: *intra*mural (literally meaning "within the walls"—this will help you keep the *intra* from becoming *inter*), *intro*spective.

OB. to, toward, against. Examples: *ob*viate, *op*ponent, *of*fer.

PER. through. Examples: *per*vasive, *per*suade.

POST. behind, after. Examples: *post*graduate, *post*ponement, *post*nasal.

PRAE. in front of. Examples: *pre*eminent, *pre*scribe, *pref*erence.

PRO. in front, for. Examples: *pro*pose, *pro*minent, *pro*mote.

RE. again, back. Examples: *re*trench, *re*cover, *re*trieve.

SUB. under, up from below, beneath. Examples: *sub*marine, *sus*pend.

SUPER. over, above. Examples: *super*ficial, *super*ior, *super*intendent.

TRANS. across, over. Examples: *trans*fer, *trans*continental.

There's no need to memorize all these words and prefixes. Just look them over now, and refer to them later if you encounter a word that you think has a Latin root. Again, check the notes in your dictionary immediately following words that give you spelling problems. If there is a Latin root, learn the root to help you remember the correct spelling.

Common Latin Words Used in English— and Tips for Spelling Them Correctly

The following Latin words serve as roots for many English words that may be hard to spell. This list is certainly not exhaustive, and I haven't even included many of the Latin-based words that we've already discussed. But I do want to encourage you to be alert to possible Latin roots when you're having trouble remembering the spelling of an English word, because focusing on the Latin can reinforce and enhance your spelling skills.

ADVERSUS. This Latin adjective, which means adverse or opposite, is the root for words like "adversary." (Note the presence of the *d*, which may be dropped in spelling errors.)

ANNUS. This Latin noun means year. English derivatives include "perennial' and "centennial." (Note the double *n*'s.)

APPELLO, APPELLARE. This Latin verb, meaning to name or call, is the basis for English words like "appellate." (Note the double *p* and double *l*.)

AUDIO, AUDIRE. This Latin verb means to hear. It's the root for English words like "inaudible" and "audition." (Note the *au* and the presence of the *i* after *d*, rather than an *e*, an *a*, or some other letter.)

BENE. This Latin adverb means well. English derivatives include "benevolence" and "benefit." (Note the two *e*'s.)

COGITO, COGITARE. The meaning is to think or mull over, and derivatives include "cogitate."

CORPUS, CORPORIS. This noun means body and is the root for English words like "corporeal" and "corporal." (Note the two *o*'s.)

DOCEO, DOCERE. This Latin verb means to teach. English words arising from it include "docile."

FEMINA. This word, which means woman, is the basis for "feminine" and other such English words.

FINIS. This word, meaning end or boundary, is the base for English words like "infinite" and "finite."

INCIPIO, INCIPERE. This Latin verb means begin. Derivatives include "incipient." (Note the presence of a *c* rather than an *s*.)

LAUDO, LAUDARE. The meaning is praise, and English words include "laudatory."

LIBRI. This Latin word means books and is the root for "library." Note the *libr* sequence of letters, in contrast with the common misspellings "libary" and "liberry."

LICET. This verb means it is permitted. English words include "license." (Note the positioning of the *c* and the *s*.)

MAGISTRI. This word is the plural of *magister* and means teachers. Derivatives include "magistrate."

MALUS. This word means evil or bad (note the single *l*). English words include "malefactor" and "malevolent."

MILLE. This word, which means 1,000, is the root for "millennium." (Note the double *l*. Also, the second part of this word is derived from *anni*, meaning "years." Note the double *n*.)

MISCEO, MISCERE. This Latin verb means to mix. English derivatives include "miscellaneous." (Note the positioning of the *sc*.)

NIHIL. This word, which means nothing, is the basis for our word "annihilate." (The English is a combination of the Latin *ad*, changed to *an*, meaning "to," and *nihil*.)

NOMEN, NOMINIS. This noun means name. It's the root for such words as "nomenclature" and "nominal." (Note that the letter following *m* may be an *e* or an *i*, depending on the word.)

NUNTIO, NUNTIARE. This verb means to report or announce. English words include "pronounce" and "pronunciation." (Many people become confused when they have to spell "pronunciation," "enunciation," or the like, primarily because the root English word "pronounce" isn't present in them. But the Latin root *is* present—and that should provide some help remembering the spelling.)

PECUNIA. This means money. English words include "impecunious" (*in* meaning not, plus *pecunia*).

QUAERO, QUAERERE. This Latin verb means to ask or to look for. English derivatives include "query" and "perquisite." (Note that the *ae* may change to *e* or *i*, depending on the word.)

SENEX, SENIS. This word, which means old, is the root for English words like "senile" and "seniority." (Note the single *n* and the presence of the *i*.)

SIMILIS, SIMILE. This adjective means similar or resembling. English derivatives include "dissimilar." (Note the two *s*'s and the single *m*. This word is derived from *dis*, meaning "not," and *similis*.)

SOLUS. This adjective means only or alone. English words include "solitary" and "solitude." (Note the single *l*.)

TENEO, TENERE. This verb means to hold. English derivatives include "tenet," "tenacious," and "tenable." (Note the single *n*.)

TERRA. This word means earth or land. Derivatives include "Mediterranean," "subterranean," and "territorial." (Note the double *r* in each of these words.)

VINCO, VINCERE. This verb means to overcome, triumph over, or conquer. English relatives include "invincible." (Note there is a *c* rather than an *s*.)

In addition to these Latin-based words, there is also a substantial segment of the English vocabulary that is derived from other foreign languages. Consider a few of these possibilities in the next section.

Other Foreign Spelling Feats

Like other listings in this book, the following is not intended to be complete. These are just some of the most common foreign words and phrases I've encountered that are frequently misspelled. Also, I've included additional Latin phrases that haven't been mentioned elsewhere.

AD HOC. Latin, meaning intended for an immediate purpose; improvised.

AD NAUSEAM. Latin, meaning to a sickening extent.

À GAUCHE. French for "on the left hand."

À LA BONNE HEURE. French for "at a good time," or "all right."

ALOHA OE. Hawaiian for "love to you" or "greetings" or "goodbye."

A MAXIMIS AD MINIMA. Latin for "from the greatest to the least."

ARS LONGA, VITA BREVIS. Latin for "art is long, life is short."

AU CONTRAIRE. French for "on the contrary."

AUTRES TEMPS, AUTRES MOEURS. French for "other times, other customs."

À VOTRE SANTÉ. French for "to your health!" This phrase may be used as a toast.

BÊTE NOIRE. French for "black beast," or something or someone greatly disliked.

BIEN ENTENDU. French for "understood" or "of course."

BON APPÉTIT. French for "good appetite" or "enjoy your food."

BONJOUR. French for "good day."

BONSOIR. French for "good evening."

CARTE BLANCHE. French for "blank document," or an ability to exercise complete power in a certain area.

CAVEAT EMPTOR. Latin for "let the buyer beware."

C'EST LA VIE. French for "that's life" or "that's the way it goes."

CHÂTEAU EN ESPAGNE. French for "castle in Spain," or far-fetched idea.

CHE SARÀ, SARÀ. Italian for "what will be, will be."

COGITO, ERGO SUM. Latin for "I think, therefore I am."

COMME CI, COMME ÇA. French for "so-so."

D'ACCORD. French for "agreed."

DOLCE VITA. Italian for "sweet life," or a life of leisure and self-satisfaction.

DOMINUS VOBISCUM. Latin for "the Lord be with you."

EN GARDE. French for "on guard."

ESPRIT DE CORPS. French for "group spirit."

ET TU, BRUTE? Latin for "you also, Brutus?" This phrase may be used to rebuke a seeming friend who has stabbed you in the back. (Shakespeare has Julius Caesar say this when he sees his friend Brutus among his assassins.)

EUREKA. Greek for "I have found it."

EX LIBRIS. Latin for "from the books (of)."

GUTEN TAG. German for "good day."

JEU DE MOTS. French for a pun, or play on words.

KINDER, KIRCHE, KÜCHE. German for "children, church, kitchen."

LABORARE EST ORARE. Latin for "to work is to pray."

LAISSEZ-FAIRE. French for "let do," allowing a person or community to function without interference or guidance.

MANO A MANO. Spanish for "hand to hand," often used to describe direct combat or competition.

N'EST-CE PAS? French for "isn't it so?"

NICHT WAHR? German for "isn't it true?"

NOBLESSE OBLIGE. French for "nobility obligates," indicating the responsibility that goes with high rank, privilege, or blessing.

NOUVEAU RICHE, *PL.:* **NOUVEAUX RICHES.** French for "new rich," or a person who has recently acquired wealth.

PAR AVION. French for "by airplane" or "airmail."

PAR EXEMPLE. French for "for example."

PAX VOBISCUM. Latin for "peace (be) with you."

PIED-À-TERRE. French for "foot to the ground," meaning a second place to live, often in an urban area.

PRO BONO PUBLICO. Latin for "for the public good," often used to describe services of a professional person donated to the community.

PRO PATRIA. Latin for "for country."

QUO VADIS? Latin for "where are you going?"

RAISON D'ÊTRE. French for "reason for being or existing."

RARA AVIS. Latin for "rare bird."

SALLE À MANGER. French for "dining room."

SEMPER FIDELIS. Latin for "always faithful," the motto of the U.S. Marines.

S'IL VOUS PLAÎT. French for "if you please."

SOUPE DU JOUR. French for "soup of the day," often spelled "soup du jour."

STATUS QUO. Latin for "state in which," meaning the existing situation.

TABULA RASA. Latin for "erased tablet," or the mind in a blank or uninfluenced state.

TEMPUS FUGIT. Latin for "time flies."

VIVE LA DIFFÉRENCE. French for "long live the difference," a comment that is usually applied to the difference between men and women.

WELTANSCHAUUNG. German for "worldview," or all-embracing philosophy of life.

WIE GEHT'S? German for "how's it going?"

WUNDERBAR. German for "wonderful."

WUNDERKIND. German for "child prodigy."

By now, you should be nearing the end of your twenty minutes with this language lesson. You certainly haven't become a Latin scholar, nor have you acquired a vast knowledge of any other foreign tongue. But it doesn't take much to become adept at using Latin and other languages as an aid in spelling many words that are in common use in English. Here's a summary of the approach that has been suggested:

- Always note the foreign roots for words that you find difficult to spell. You can locate a reference to the roots in the parenthetical information immediately following the word in a good dictionary.

- Reflect on the Latin or other foreign components that are present in your tough word. You'll often be reminded of some of the points that have been made about the construction of such words in this chapter. You may recognize some of the words and prefixes we've discussed, and you may even identify some of the verb forms.

- Even if you don't recognize anything familiar about the information on the roots of the word, see if you can use some of that information as a memory device to help you with the spelling.

For example, you may know nothing about ancient Greek. But if you have trouble with "philosophy," you might note that the Greek root is *philo,* meaning "friend" or "lover," and *sophia,* meaning "wisdom." Just breaking the word down this way and attaching some outside meaning to the two components will help you recall the spelling.

This completes your twenty-minute course in Latin (and other languages)—and I trust you at least have a few tools that will assist you in your spelling. Now, let's return to the mother tongue, English.

5
Double Trouble

Some of the greatest spelling problems arise when the writer is trying to decide whether to double a letter or leave it single. Many people hesitate over a relatively simple word like "disappear." Is that the right way to spell it, or should it be "dissappear," or "disapear," or maybe "dissapear"? In this case, the first version,"disappear," is correct, but how can you remember words with double letters? Are there any rules that we can apply to resolve this dilemma?

There a few rules that can be helpful. But as with most other issues in English spelling, there are always exceptions to any rule. To show you how to overcome various types of "double trouble," I'll pose several double-trouble challenges that you may confront as a speller—and at the same time, provide you with some tactics to deal with them.

Situation 1:
Double Trouble at the Beginning of a Word

Many spelling mistakes are made because the writer gets confused by a prefix—the letters that are often tacked onto the beginning of a word to change its meaning. Specifically, the last letter in a prefix may be incorrectly dropped, or an unnecessary letter may be added.

The general rule for spelling words with a prefix is this: *Use ONLY the prefix plus the base.* Don't be tempted to insert extra letters—or to drop letters that would give you too few for your prefix and base.

At the beginning of this chapter, I mentioned the word "disappear." The prefix in this word is *dis-*, meaning "apart" or "not," and the base is "appear." Breaking the word down this way and examining the meaning of the component parts makes it easier to spell the word, doesn't it? Such an analysis will prevent you from adding an extra *s,* which would erroneously change the components of the word into "*dis-*" and "sappear." (You'll recognize *dis-* from our discussion of Latin in the previous chapter.)

If you know the spelling of the prefix—a relatively easy task—you can often see how it fits onto the base word. Distinguishing the prefix from the base can do wonders for anyone's spelling by preventing incorrect use of double or single letters.

Common prefixes which can have a direct impact on the use of double or single letters include ad-, com-, in-, and re-. You've already been introduced to these in the previous chapter, but here's a more detailed discussion.

AD- (or variations such as *ac-, ar-, ag-,* or *ap-*). This prefix, which means "to" or "in addition," may be found in such words as "aggravate," "assimiliation," "address," "adhere," and "admission." As you can see from these few illustrations, the second letter in *ad-* may change to match the first letter of the base word.

Usually, spellers don't have a problem knowing what letter to use just after the first *a.* Their problem is knowing *how many* of those letters to use. All you have to remember is that where the prefix is *ad-* or one of its variations, you spell the word *only* with the two-letter prefix, plus the base.

COM- (or variations such as *con-, cor-,* or *col-*). This prefix, which means "with" or "together," appears in such words as "commit," "concede," "corroborate," and "collaborate." As you can see, there is only a single *n* in "concede" because the prefix is *con-* and the base the "cede." If you double the *n,* you'll end up with an unnecessary letter that does not go with either the prefix or the base. (Note: The word "unnecessary" that I've just used is another illustration. This can be a tough word to spell unless you analyze the word by identifying its prefix and base. The prefix is *un-* and the base is "necessary.")

On the other hand, there are *double* letters in "corroborate" and "collaborate" because the prefixes are *cor-* and *col-* and the bases also begin with an *r* and an *l,* respectively. If you drop one of these double letters, you'll violate either the prefix or the base.

DIS- (or variations such as *dif-*). This prefix means "not" or "apart," and may be found in words like "dissimilar," "differential," "dismiss," and "dissatisfaction."

Again, you can see that if you separate the prefix from the base, you'll have little trouble with these spellings. But those who fail to identify the prefix and the base may use incorrect spellings such as "disimilar," "disatisfaction," and "dissmissed."

IN- (or variations such as *im-, ir-,* or *il-*). This prefix, which may mean "in" or "not," depending on the use, appears in such words as "innovation," "inoculate," "innocuous," "immense," and "illiterate." If you know the prefix and the base in these and other potentially tough words, you'll be much more likely to get the spelling right.

RE-. This prefix, which means "again" or "back," can be especially tricky when it's hooked up with a base that begins with an *e.* For example, it's easy to misspell words like "reemphasis," "reestablish," "reestimate," "reevaluate," and "reexamination" because somehow the extra *e* just doesn't look right. But if you break down each of these words into prefix and base, you'll see that the double *e* is logical, and in fact, without it, the word doesn't make sense!

There are a number of other prefixes you may encounter, such as *mis-, per-, sub-,* and the like. The main point for spellers is that you should always identify the prefix first. Then identify the base. Finally, put them together— *without* adding any extra letters, *or* dropping necessary letters required by either the prefix or the base. If you follow these simple guidelines, you should be able to handle most of the double trouble you face at the beginning of words.

Situation 2:
Double Trouble in the Middle of a Word

Now, let's move to the middle of words that often give trouble with double or single letters. The middle part of words tends to be the hardest when it comes to deciding whether to double or not double a letter. But there are a few principles that can make spelling these words an easier task.

Examine the base.
By definition, the double trouble that occurs in the middle of a word concerns the base, or the main part of the word. If you determine that you're dealing with the base, rather than a prefix or a suffix (a word ending), then you may find that the solution is quite easy.

Take our original word, "disappear." The base is "appear," and most people would find they know how to spell that word if they separate it from the prefix *dis-*. But failing to work separately with the base may result in "disapear" or "dissapear."

Another word that is commonly misspelled is "accommodate." Either a *c* or an *m* is dropped. If you first divide it into prefix and base, you'll take care of the problem with the double *c* because it will become obvious that the word has two essential components, *ac-* and "commodate." Then, if you look closely at the base, you'll probably see that it makes more sense to double the *m* than to make it single. Related words like "commode," "commodious," or "commodity" may come to mind to help you remember the correct spelling.

Note the foreign root.
As a mnemonic device, examine the Latin or other foreign root of the word in the dictionary, as described in the previous chapter. Knowing the root will help you get the double or single letter right.

Use other associations to help your memory.
In Chapter 2, we covered the Toughest 228 words to spell, and in the descriptions of spelling techniques, we talked about seeing other words inside the main word, or making associations that arise naturally from the sound of the word. This approach can help with double trouble.

Take the word "harass." A common misspelling is "harrass." This mistake can be avoided by thinking that the word contains a cheer, "*Ha-ra*h!" Or you might also think, "Harass" *doesn't* contain a "*Harry*."

Situation 3:
Double Trouble at the End of a Word

Double trouble at the end of a word usually involves (1) action words, or verbs, ending in a consonant (any letter other than *a, e, i, o, u,* or *y*), and (2) endings that begin with a vowel, such as *-ing* or *-ed*. The big question in such cases is this: When I add the ending, should I double the final consonant or keep it single?

To illustrate, consider the words "disappear," "happen," "rivet," "desist," "defer," "expel," "travel," and "worship." If you add *-ing* to each of these words, you end up with these results:

DISAPPEARING	DEFERRING
HAPPENING	EXPELLING
RIVETING	TRAVELING *OR* TRAVELLING
DESISTING	WORSHIPING *OR* WORSHIPPING

Why are there these variations? A simple set of guidelines should help you understand. *All* of the following requirements must be met for a final consonant to be doubled.

Requirement 1: Emphasis on the last syllable

First, you should identify where the emphasis or accent is placed in sounding the word. For a final consonant to be doubled, the *emphasis must be on the final syllable.*

Another way to remember this is to think in these terms: More of a final emphasis may add "weight" to the word that requires more final letters to create a balance. It may help to imagine that when the emphasis comes at the end of the word, the word begins to tip to one side or the other; consequently, it needs more letters to "hold it up," or support it when a suffix is added.

You'll note that the words "defer" and "expel" have the accent on the last syllable, and their final consonant is doubled when the *-ing* is added. The extra *r* and *l* help to balance the final accent.

In contrast, "happen" and "rivet" have the accent on the first syllable. So they use only a single consonant with the -*ing*. In effect, they remain in balance and don't need the extra "weight" of the doubled letter.

Finally, because single-syllable words like "sit" automatically have the accent on the last syllable, they qualify for a doubling of the final consonant, as can be seen in a word like "sitting."

But this is not the whole story. Look at "desisting." This word has the emphasis on the final syllable, but the final consonant *isn't* doubled with -*ing*. Why not? Read on to solve the mystery.

Requirement 2: Only one final consonant

Another condition of doubling the final consonant is that the word must end in only one consonant. To follow our balancing image a step further, you might say that the extra consonant at the end—even though it's not the same as the final consonant—adds the extra "weight" that's required to offset the -*ing*. Therefore, no doubling is required.

So "desist," because it has *two* final consonants, *s* and *t*, doesn't need an extra *t* when the form changes to "desisting" or "desisted." (A single-syllable verb such as "lack" is in the same boat. The -*ing* form is "lacking," with a single *k*, because the word ends in two consonants.)

Requirement 3: Only one vowel immediately before the final consonant

Still another necessary condition for doubling the final consonant is that there can only be one vowel immediately preceding the last letter. Two or more in a row will eliminate the word. "Disappear" has *two* vowels immediately before the final *r,* and so we spell "disappearing" with only one *r.*

As you can see, after applying all these tests, we're now left with two words that require a doubling of the final consonant, "deferring" and "expelling." But what about "traveling/travelling" and "worshiping/worshipping"? With these two words, the emphasis is placed on the first, not the last, syllable. They do meet the other two conditions, but that shouldn't be enough to justify the doubled-consonant spelling, should it?

Actually, the preferred spelling for both is to use a single final consonant. The fact that a second, double-letter ending is acceptable is just a quirk in the way our language has developed. (You'll find that a number of other words, such as "benefited-benefitted," fall into this category.)

Some additional points might be added to fine-tune these rules. For example, for a letter to be doubled the added ending should begin with a vowel, as do *-ing, -ed,* and *-ence.* Also, if the emphasis in the word is changed from the final syllable to another syllable when the ending is added (as happens when "refer" becomes "reference"), the consonant is not doubled.

But these qualifications may complicate matters for the ordinary speller more than they help. For most purposes, the above three guidelines are all you'll need to stay out of double trouble at the end of words.

Now, let's turn to a particularly deadly topic that plagues the terrible speller—the enemy I've called the "silent assassins."

6
Silent Assassins

Silent assassins are those letters that are lethal to good spelling because they remain hidden in words. Either they are not pronounced at all, or if they are pronounced, it's often with an unusual sound.

For example, the *e* in words like "noticeable," "serviceable," and "ninety" will often be overlooked and may deliver a lethal jab to the reputation of a good speller. The *h* in "khaki" is another killer, along with the *h* in "diarrhea" and "hemorrhage."

The Vice President of the United States, Dan Quayle, was stabbed by one of these assassins in 1992, when he erroneously instructed a sixth-grader participating in a spelling bee to add an *e* to "potato." In fact, the plural of "potato" is "potatoes," with a silent *e*. But with the singular, there is no *e*.

Don't heap too much scorn on Quayle or others who trip over a word like "potato." It's easy to make mistakes with your *e*'s—unless you keep a few basic principles in mind.

Warding Off the Final-*e* Attack

Many people erroneously *add* an *e* because they're unsure about whether or not it belongs there—and also they're confused because they know the *e* will be silent. So they mistakenly write "tomatoe" instead of "tomato." Or they spell "envelope," meaning the holder for a letter, as "envelop," a verb meaning to encompass or enclose.

The best way to avoid this mistake is to remember that as a general rule, nouns in the singular like "potato" and "tomato" should have no final *e*. (But of course there are exceptions, such as "envelope"!)

Plurals may also present you with some silent *e* problems. It's sometimes necessary to add an *e* when you refer to more than one of an item. But in most cases, the ending will be *-os*. The best way to remember when to use the less common *-oes* form is just to memorize the following words, which are frequently used in business or personal writing:

ECHOES	TOMATOES
EMBARGOES	TORPEDOES
POTATOES	VETOES

According to current dictionary entries, you are required to use *-oes* in creating the plural of these seven words. With most other nouns ending in *o*—such as "tornado," "motto," and "mosquito"—you can either include the *e* or omit it in forming the plural.

Before we leave the *e* in plurals, let me say something about a special word, "hero." The plural for "hero" when it means a famous, legendary, or admirable figure is "heroes." But the plural of the word when it means the sandwich is "heros."

Buried Letters

Sometimes the silent assassin may lurk in the middle part of a word. In "noticeable," "serviceable," and "interchangeable," for instance, the middle *e* may thwart the unwary.

How can you tell when to keep the *e* in words like these? Generally speaking, when you have a soft *c*, soft *g*, or other soft sound just before the *e*, you should keep the *e*. With hard sounds, you drop it. In the above examples, the *c* before the *e* sounds soft, like an *s* (rather than a *k*, which would be a hard sound), and the *g* sounds soft, like a *j*.

Of course, the assassin doesn't have to be an *e*. Any letter that isn't pronounced can create problems. Consider the *i* in "business," or the *h* in "khaki," or the *h* in "diarrhea" or "hemorrhage."

Unfortunately, for many of these silent letters there are no consistent rules or guidelines that will help you remember the correct spelling. Consequently, the best technique is to fall back on strategies such as those described in Chapters 1 and 2.

1. *Mis*pronounce the word to help you remember the silent letter.
2. Use odd or memorable associations or visual images.

3. Picture the correct spelling of the word in your mind. Actually *see* that silent letter that gives you so much trouble.

When Assassins Strike at the Beginning

Some of the most frustrating words to spell are those with silent letters that reside in the lead-off position. Words like "mnemonic," "gnostic," "gnaw," "gnash," and "knack" may not only be hard to spell; they can be hard to pronounce as well!

The tendency is to want to pull the silent letter or letters into the pronunciation. When that happens, the number of syllables may increase, or the other letters may become scrambled. The best and simplest approach to these insidious letters is just to tell yourself, "I'm *not* going to pronounce that silent letter—I'm going to start with the *next* letter." If you do this, the pronunciation *and* spelling of the words should become rather easy. Then, to recall the fact that you're omitting the silent letter in your pronunciation, just make a discreet note to yourself about the letter's presence.

Here are a couple of illustrations:

With "knack," tell yourself, "The pronunciation of this word is 'nack,' but it begins with a silent *k*."

With "gnostic," tell yourself, "The pronunciation of this word is 'nostic,' but it begins with a silent *g*."

These silent assassins can appear in many different guises and locations in words. In other contexts, we've already considered words like "Wednesday," with its silent *d*, and "Philippines," with the *f* sound at the beginning and the dilemma of whether to use one *l* or a double *p*. (It could be argued that the second *p* in the double *p* is one of our silent assassins.)

You'll often find that none of the rules or guidelines we've discussed so far can be applied perfectly to help you deal with a silent letter. So you'll just have to fall back on one of the memory devices, such as mispronunciation, odd associations, or mental pictures. And in the last analysis, that's not such a bad approach. *Most* English words don't fit neatly into a certain spelling rule, and so the more firmly you can nail an individual word down in your memory, the more likely you'll be to spell it correctly later.

The silent assassin problem may also lurk in other spelling issues, such as the final endings to words, as we'll see in the next chapter.

7
The End Game

In some ways, we've saved the hardest spelling problems for last. The endings of words, or suffixes, create more difficulties for many people than all the other challenges of spelling combined.

Many people hesitate over "apparent." (Should it be "apparant"?) Or "dependent." (Should it be "dependant"?) Or "readable." (Should it be "readible"? Or "superintendent." (Should it be "superintendant"?) Or "canoeing." (Should it be "canoing"?) Or "irresistible." (Should it be "irresistable"?) Or "lashes." (Should it be "lashs"?)

In each of the above cases, the version of the word listed first is correct. But it's hard for almost anyone to get these and similar tough endings right all of the time. How can you master the end game of spelling? You'll be well on your way after we've considered the following major topics:

- A plethora of plurals and apostrophes
- The art of changing *y* to *i*

- The *ance-ence* issue
- The *ible-able* puzzle
- The kinship of *ly* and *ally*

A Plethora of Plurals and Apostrophes

Plurals, or words that refer to more than one of a thing, can create all sorts of problems for spellers—especially when they involve what is known as "irregular" plurals, or when they become mixed up with apostrophes.

To help you keep things straight, here are a few simple guidelines to bear in mind (I say "guidelines" because there are too many exceptions and variations to dub the following points "rules"):

THE SIMPLE *S*
The plurals of most words are formed by adding only an *s*. Examples: "girls," "trains," "hats."

THE *ES* VARIATION
The plurals of some words are formed by adding *es*. You can usually tell by the distinct, separate sound at the end of the word whether or not *es* is appropriate. Just pronounce the plural as you normally would, and you'll probably immediately know whether you need the *es*. Examples:

The plural of "boss" is "bosses." You can hear the separate *es* sound—and it would be very odd to have a triple *s*.

The plural of "latch" is "latches." Again, you can hear the *es*.

The plural of "tax" is "taxes." You wouldn't say "taxs" because you'd lose that separate *es* sound.

The plural of "lash" is "lashes." This one is a little tougher because it might be possible to slip in a separate sound with "lashs." But the clear, distinct extra sound is only possible with *es*.

Note: The same principles apply with many verbs. You usually add a simple *s* when you're using the third person: "He runs." But when the distinct *es* sound is present, you add the extra letter: "He searches."

THE *F* WORDS

When you make the plural of words that end in *f* or *fe*, confusion may reign—because there is really no rhyme nor reason to the way the endings are formed.

Sometimes you just add an *s* to the *f*, as in "reefs" and "chiefs." Other times, the *f* must be changed to *ves*, as in "sheaves" and "shelves."

And then, there are those words that allow you to make the plural either way. These include "hoof," the plural of which may be spelled "hoofs" or "hooves," and "handkerchief," the plural of which may be spelled "handkerchiefs" or "handkerchieves." (I continue to puzzle over why the plural of "chief" must be "chiefs," while the derivative word "handkerchief" can go either way.)

In the last analysis, there are two ways to deal successfully with the spelling of the *f* words. First, you must learn to rely on your reaction to the sound of the plurals. The chances are, the correct spelling will sound better to you.

It just doesn't sound quite right to say "believes" when you're talking about more than one "belief," does it? "Believes" *is* a correct verb form, as in "she believes in all the right things." But it's *not* a correct way to make the plural of the noun "belief." The form "beliefs" is the only way to do that.

Another example of this sound test is a made-up word like "themselfs." The only correct way to form this plural is "themselves," and that's the only correct spelling that sounds right.

In addition to the sound test, with many irregular spellings in English you'll have to rely on memory devices for the *f* plurals. For example, to remember that the plural of "chief" is "chiefs," you might say to yourself, "the *f* in the plural means that a chie*f* is *f*irst."

WEIRD WORDS

The plurals of a number of words like "child," "foot," "tooth," and "chairman" are formed in unusual ways. In these cases, the plurals are "children," "feet," "teeth," and "chairmen."

Other words have unusual plurals because they have been taken from a foreign language. The plural for "criterion" is "criteria"; for "crisis" is "crises"; and for "phenomenon" is "phenomena."

How do you remember these strange variations? There are no consistent rules. You'll just have to note the irregular plurals that give you trouble and memorize them.

The Art of Changing *y* to *i*

Whenever a noun ends in *y*, and the *y* is preceded by a consonant, the plural is formed by changing the *y* to an *i* and adding *es*.

Examples: The plural of "body" is "bodies." The plural of "lady" is "ladies."

But don't be tricked by that ending *y*. A consonant must come before the *y*; otherwise, you just add an *s* for the plural. Thus the plural of "way" is "ways," and the plural of "attorney" is "attorneys."

Finally, even if a proper noun, such as "Larry," ends in *y* and is preceded by a consonant, you usually just add the *s*, as in "Larrys" (meaning more than one man named Larry). You *wouldn't* write "Larries."

When a word ends in *y* and you want to add an ending other than a plural ending, you'll almost always change the *y* to an *i unless* the ending itself begins with an *i*.

Here are some illustrations: The word "twenty" becomes "twentieth" (the *y* is changed to *i* when the ending *eth* is added). The word "defy" becomes "defiance." *But* the verb "try" becomes "trying," because the ending *ing* begins with an *i*.

The *ance-ence* Issue

Now, we arrive at one of the hardest spelling problems in English. When do you use the ending *ance* or *ence*, which sound alike?

Some have tried to trace the answer to these problems

back to the Latin roots of English words. Among other things, they may try to analyze how the infinitives of different verbs are formed. You may recall that some verbs end in *are*, some in *ere*, some in *ire*, and some in other letters. But even if you return to the Latin roots, the answers in English aren't always clear or consistent. So forget the Latin.

Although there are no consistent rules to help you with these endings, there is a technique that may provide you with some assistance. I call this the "Similarity Secret."

It goes like this: When you encounter a word with one of these endings and you find you just can't recall the correct spelling, try thinking of another, similar ending for the same root that gives you less trouble. For example, you may never be able to remember that "dependent" is spelled with an *ent*, but you may be able to remember the spelling of "dependence." In this case, all you have to do is take the *e* in the *ence* ending and transfer it to "dependent." In every case that matters, you'll find you have the correct spelling.

The *ible-able* Puzzle

A number of experts have tried to devise complex guidelines for spelling the words that end in *ible* or *able*. And if you're willing to memorize all these detailed rules, they can help. But most people don't have the time or inclination to figure out every "ible-able" variation.

So I'd suggest you keep it simple with these two thoughts:

THOUGHT 1

First, if you add the ending to a complete word—or a word that is complete except for a final *e*—use the *able* ending. Examples: "marketable," "readable," and "understandable." Some words, like "collectible" and "collectable," may be spelled either way.

But if the ending is added to an incomplete word, use the *ible* ending. Examples: "intangible" "legible," and "incorrigible."

But be aware there are plenty of exceptions. Words like "capable" and "inequitable" aren't complete words, yet they have *able* endings.

Also, the Similarity Secret often doesn't work with these endings. For example, "resistance" is the correct spelling of one variation of the base word "resist." But so is "resistible." So when you're confronted with an "ible-able" puzzle, don't rely too heavily on the Similarity Secret.

THOUGHT 2

Focus on those ten or fifteen *ible-able* words that give you the most trouble and memorize them. Use the memory techniques we've already discussed in Chapters 1 and 2.

The Kinship of *ly* and *ally*

Finally, we arrive at a concept that is usually fairly easy to apply. When you add *ly* to a word, you first form the entire word, and *only then* add the *ly*.

Examples: "entirely," "accidentally," and "occasionally." As you can see, you begin each of these with an entire base word—"entire," "accidental," and "occasional"—

and only then add the *ly*. A mistake that's often made with base words that end in *al* is to drop that *al* before adding the *ly*. So you might end up with "accidently" or "occasionly"—which are incorrect.

Note: Some words, such as "truly," require you to drop the final *e*. In this case, "true" becomes "tru," which is not a complete word. You'll just have to memorize these exceptions.

There is a close relationship between the *ly* words and other words that require the ending *ally* with words that didn't originally end in *al*. Some illustrations of these are "sporadically," "automatically" and "basically."

One rule of thumb that works to some extent with these words is to note that they tend to end in *ic*. As usual, however, there are exceptions: Some words, such as "frantically" (or "franticly") can be spelled either way, while at least one common word, "publicly," must be spelled with only an *ly*.

There are a number of other things we might mention about the End Game of spelling. One is that you don't have to worry much about whether to end a word in *ify* or *efy*, because in almost every case, the correct answer will be *ify*. Those that end in *efy*, such as "stupefy," aren't in common use in ordinary correspondence or writing, and so there's really no need to worry about them. Just try to become familiar with the most important and frequently encountered End Game principles that have been discussed. This preparation is all you'll need to improve your spelling significantly.

8
A Celebration of Competence

As I indicated at the beginning of this book, my intention has not been to transform you into a spelling-bee champion. *I'm* not a spelling-bee champ. Many of us begin as Terrible Spellers, and we continue to struggle with many words, even after we improve beyond the lowest category of performance.

The purpose of this book has been to help the Terrible Speller become a Competent Speller—a person who spells *most* words right. When Competent Spellers miss, they're often in good company with their colleagues and bosses.

You're not supposed to remember all the rules and exceptions I've mentioned. In fact, I've tried to keep the rules and guidelines to a minimum because a heavy reliance on that approach simply won't work with most people. It's best just to identify a few major areas of weakness in your spelling and then concentrate on improving those deficiencies.

As part of an ongoing program to improve your spelling in the future—and to be sure that you don't just lay this book aside and never use the principles in it again—I'd suggest the following approach:

STEP 1
Identify the twenty words that give you the most difficulty, and memorize their spellings.

Use the memory-enhancing techniques mentioned in Chapters 1 and 2. Really *nail* those twenty words! If you do, you'll probably find that your spelling will become better immediately.

STEP 2
Identify the five rules or guidelines mentioned in the previous chapters that are toughest for you to apply, and become an expert in those areas.

Some people have a great deal of trouble remembering the techniques for doubling or not doubling the final single consonant in a word when a suffix, or ending, is added. Is it "deferring" or "defering"? Is it "occurring" or "occuring"? Is it "hindering" or "hinderring"? Is it "shopping" or "shoping"? Is it "drooping" or "drooping"?

In each of the above cases, the first version is the correct spelling. To be right every time, or almost every time, all you have to do is learn to wield the doubling rule.

The word "wield" brings up another common error—the placement of *i* before or after *e*. Again, if you learn the rule, along with its various exceptions, you'll know the correct spellings are "wield," "weird," "perceive," "foreign," and "believe."

You don't have to memorize every rule mentioned in

this book or any other book. Just pick those five guidelines that give you the most trouble and specialize in them.

STEP 3
Practice the memory techniques that appeal to you the most.

Again, don't try to become a world-class memory expert. Just pick a few methods that come naturally to you and will help your memory in spelling *and* in other areas of your life.

You may find that making use of absurd associations helps you attach the faces of people to their names. So, when you're introduced to a Mary McBride, you might think, "She reminds me of a merry bride." Then picture the woman as an uproariously happy bride, complete with bridal gown and silly smile. This same approach will help you remember the spelling of a word like "dissipate," which you might picture as a personified *dish*, complete with face and arms, that *sips* cider and *ate* a huge meal.

STEP 4
Buy a spiral notebook and keep a running list of the words that give you trouble.

You won't remember all the words you have difficulty spelling as you read this book. Some will come to mind later, when you struggle to write a letter or report. You'll develop more quickly into a Competent Speller if you are systematic in keeping track of those words that give you the most problems.

STEP 5

Develop a dictionary habit.

Most people refer to the dictionary only rarely. You should transform yourself into one who constantly combs the dictionary. If you have a serious doubt about a word and you have the time, look it up!

If every Terrible Speller would follow this approach, there would be no Terrible Spellers—or at least, no one would be able to identify them. A failure to look a word up is usually a reflection of laziness, not a lack of time. If you really care what people think about you, if you're interested in having them regard you as intelligent and literate, then you should buy a couple of good single-volume dictionaries, one for home and one for work, and *use* them.

Just following these five steps and then returning to them periodically to refresh your memory and your skills will enable you to improve dramatically. Don't believe those who say, with some resignation, "Some people are born spellers, and others like me aren't." That's not so! Only a few may be so gifted that they have the potential to win contests. But *everyone* can increase his or her expertise as a speller.

Dramatic improvement is within your grasp at this very moment. Seize the opportunity, and leave the depressing realm of Terrible Spellerdom forever behind! Prepare to celebrate your entry into the kingdom of Competent Spellers!

APPENDIX

A List of the Most Commonly Misspelled Words Used in Everyday Writing

A

ABHOR

ABSCESS

ABUNDANT

ACCEDE (to express approval or consent, see "exceed")

ACCELERATE

ACCEPT (to receive; see "except")

ACCESSORY

ACCOMMODATE

ACCOMPANY

ACCUMULATE

ACETIC (sour; see "ascetic")

ACKNOWLEDGE

ACKNOWLEDGEABLE

ACKNOWLEDGING

ACQUIESCE

ADDENDUM

ADDRESS

ADJACENT

ADJUDICATE

ADMISSIBLE

ADOLESCENCE

ADRENALIN (trademark)

ADRENALINE

ADULTERY

ADVERSE (acting against; see "averse")

ADVERTISE

ADVISER OR ADVISOR

AESTHETIC OR ESTHETIC

AFFECT (to influence; see "effect")

AGGRAVATE

AGGRESSION

AGRICULTURE

AID (act of helping; see "aide")

AIDE (an assistant; see "aid")

AISLE (passage between seats)

À LA CARTE

ALBUQUERQUE

ALLELUIA *OR* HALLELUJAH

ALLOT

ALL READY (prepared)

ALL RIGHT

ALLSPICE

ALLUDE (to make indirect reference; see "elude")

ALLUSION (act of alluding or hinting at; see "illusion")

A LOT (not "alot")

ALTAR (raised table for worship; see "alter")

ALTER (to change; see "altar")

ALUMNA, *PL.* ALUMNAE

ALUMNUS, *PL.* ALUMNI

AMATEUR

AMEND (to change for the better; see "emend")

ANALYSIS, *PL.* ANALYSES

ANALYZE

ANCHOR

ANECDOTE (short, amusing story; see "antidote")

ANNIHILATE

ANNIVERSARY

ANNUAL

ANNUL

ANOINT

ANSWER

ANTECEDENT

ANTIDOTE (a remedy; see "anecdote")

ANTIQUE

ANTISEPTIC

APERTURE

APOSTROPHE

APPALL (also appal)

APPAREL

APPARENT

APPETITE

APPRAISE (to set a value on; see "apprise")

APPRISE (to notify; see "appraise")

APROPOS

ARROGANT

ASCERTAIN

ASCETIC (austere;

characterized by giving up luxuries; see "acetic")

ASSESS

ASTERISK

ATHLETE

ATROCITY

ATTENTION

AUDIBLE

AU LAIT (French for "with milk")

AU NATUREL

AUTUMN

AVALANCHE

AVERSE (having a feeling of distaste or repugnance; see "adverse")

AWESOME

AWRY

B

BACCALAUREATE

BACHELOR

BADMINTON

BALLOON

BANAL

BANANA

BAPTISM

BAPTIZE

BARBECUE

BATHE

BATTALION

BAZAAR (market; see "bizarre")

BEGGAR

BEIGE

BELLIGERENT

BELLWETHER

BENEFACTOR

BENIGN

BERSERK

BIANNUAL (occurring twice a year; see "biennial")

BICYCLE

BIENNIAL (occurring once in two years; see "biannual")

BIZARRE (strange; see "bazaar")

BOISTEROUS

BOLOGNA

BONA FIDE

BOOTEE OR BOOTIE (baby's knitted boot; see "booty")

BOOTY (plunder; see "bootee")

BOUDOIR

BOUILLON (clear soup; see "bullion")

BOURGEOIS (middle-class)

BRAILLE

BRASSIERE

BREATH (exhaled air; see "breathe")

BREATHE (to inhale; see "breath")

BRETHREN

BRITAIN (country; see "Briton")

BRITON (citizen of Great Britain; see "Britain")

BROACH (to open; see "brooch")

BROCCOLI

BROOCH (decorative pin; see "broach")

BRUISE

BRUSQUE

BUCCANEER

BUCOLIC

BUDGET

BUFFET

BULLION (uncoined gold or silver; see "bouillon")

BURGLAR

BUSINESS

BYLAW OR BYELAW

BYLINE

BYPASS

BY-PRODUCT

BYTE (computer digits)

BYWORD

C

CACHE (hiding place; see "cachet")

CACHET (indication of approval; see "cache")

CAFÉ AU LAIT

CAFETERIA

CAFFEINE

CALENDAR (time schedule)

CALIFORNIA

CALISTHENICS

CALLOUS (hard or insensitive; see "callus")

CALLUS (hardened skin; see "callous")

CAMARADERIE

CAMOUFLAGE

CAMPAIGN

CANDIDATE

CATALOUPE OR CANTALOUP

CAPITAL (city serving as seat of government; money or assets; see "capitol")

CAPITOL (building housing state legislature; see "capital")

CAPITOL (building housing U.S. Congress)

CARIBBEAN

CAROL (song of joy or mirth; see "carrel")

CAROUSEL (merry-go-round)

CARREL (enclosed table; see "carol")

CARTE BLANCHE

CARTILAGE

CATALYST

CATASTROPHE

CATEGORY

CEDE (to yield or grant)

CELEBRATE

CELEBRITY

CELLOPHANE

CEMETERY

CENSER (incense holder; see "censor" and "censure")

CENSOR (one who oversees public conduct and morals; see "censer" and "censure")

CENSURE (an official reprimand; see "censer" and "censor")

CEREBRAL

CHAFE (to irritate)

CHAISE LONGUE

CHAMPAGNE (wine; see "champaign")

CHAMPAIGN (open country; see "champagne")

CHANDELIER

CHAOS

CHASM

CHASSIS

CHAUFFEUR

CHOCOLATE

CHOLESTEROL

CHOOSE

CHOSE (past tense of "choose")

CIGARETTE

CIRCUIT

CIRCUMSTANCE

CIRRHOSIS

CITE (to summon; to quote; see "sight" and "site")

CLANDESTINE

CLARET

CLASSIFY

CLEANSE

CLEARANCE

CLICHÉ

CLIQUE

COALESCE

COARSE (rough)

COAUTHOR

COCOA

CODICIL

COERCE

COGNAC

COIFFEUR (hairdresser; see "coiffure")

COIFFURE (hairstyle; see "coiffeur")

COINCIDE

COLLABORATE

COLLEAGUE

COLONEL (military officer)

COLUMN

COMEBACK (sharp or witty reply; a recovery)

COME BACK (to return to life or vitality)

COMMEMORATE

COMMENSURATE

COMMITTEE

COMMUNICATE

COMPLEMENT (that which completes; see "compliment")

COMPLIMENT (expression of esteem; see "complement")

COMPRISE

CONCEDE

CONCIERGE

CONCILIATORY

CONCISE

CONCOCT

CONDEMN

CONDESCEND

CONDOMINIUM

CONFIDANT, CONFIDANTE (one to whom secrets are entrusted; see "confident")

CONFIDENT (self-assured; see "confidant")

CONJUGAL

CONNECTICUT

CONNOISSEUR

CONSCIENCE

CONSCIOUS

CONSISTENT

CONSTITUENT

CONSTITUTE

CONSUL (foreign representative; see "council" and "counsel")

CONSUMMATE

CONTEMPORARY

CONTENTIOUS

CONVALESCE

COORDINATE

CORESPONDENT (adulterer; see "correspondent")

COROLLARY

CORPORATE

CORRESPOND

CORRESPONDENT (letter writer; journalist in a distant place; see "corespondent")

CORROBORATE

COUNCIL (an assembly; see "consul" and "counsel")

COUNSEL (advice or attorney; see "consul" and "council")

COUP D'ÉTAT

CREATE

CREDENCE

CREDIBLE

CREDULITY

CRESCENDO

CRITERION, *PL.* CRITERIA

CRITICIZE

CURRANT (small raisin; see "current")

CURRENT (at the present time; electricity; see "currant")

CURRICULUM, *PL.* CURRICULA

CYLINDER

D

DACHSHUND

DAREDEVIL

DAUGHTER

DEACON

DEADLINE

DECEITFUL

DECEIVE

DECIMAL

DEDICATE

DEDUCTIBLE

DEFERENCE (respect due a superior)

DEFERMENT

DEFERRED

DEFINITE

DEIGN

DELECTABLE

DELICACY

DELINEATE

DELUXE

DEODORANT

DEPENDABLE

DEPENDENT

DESERT (arid, barren land; just reward; see "dessert")

DESPERATE (having lost hope; see "disparate")

DESSERT (sweet food at end of meal; see "desert")

DETERIORATE

DETRIMENT

DEVASTATE

DEVOUR

DIAGNOSE

DIALOGUE OR DIALOG

DIAPHRAGM

DIARRHEA

DIASTOLIC

DICTIONARY

DIPLOMACY

DISAPPEAR

DISASSEMBLE

DISCIPLE

DISCIPLINE

DISCOMFIT

DISCOMFORT

DISCREET (showing good judgment; see "discrete")

DISCRETE (distinct or separate; see "discreet")

DISILLUSION

DISK OR DISC

DISPARAGE

DISPARATE (dissimilar or different)

DISPEL

DISPELLED

DISPENSE

DISSATISFIED

DISSECT

DISSEMBLE

DISSEMINATE

DISSENT (difference of opinion)

DISSOCIATE (to separate from association with another)

DISTILL OR DISTIL

DISTINCT

DOMICILE

DONOR

DOUGH (mixture of flour or meal)

DRINKABLE

DROUGHT

DRUDGERY

DYSENTERY

E

EATABLE

ECSTASY

EDIBLE

EFFECT (to bring about; result; see "affect")

EFFICIENT

ELICIT (to draw forth; see "illicit")

ELUDE (to evade; see "allude")

EMANATE

EMBARRASS

EMEND (to correct by

textual alterations; see "amend")

EMIGRATE (to move out of; see "immigrate")

EMINENT (important; see "immanent" and "imminent")

EMPHASIZE

ENCLOSE

ENCOMPASS

ENCYCLOPEDIA

ENDORSEMENT

ENLARGE

ENROLL OR ENROL

ENTHRALL OR ENTHRAL

ENTREPRENEUR

ENUMERATE

ENVELOP (to enclose; see "envelope")

ENVELOPE (container for letter; see "envelop")

ENZYME

EPHEMERAL

EPISCOPAL

EPISCOPALIAN

EPISODE

ESTHETIC OR AESTHETIC

ESTIMATE

ET CETERA

EUPHEMISM

EVANGELISM

EXACERBATE

EXAGGERATE

EXCEED (to extend outside of; see "accede")

EXCEL

EXCELLED

EXCEPT (to take or leave out; but for; see "accept")

EXCERPT

EXCITABLE

EXCITE

EXCITEMENT

EXERCISE

EXHILARATE

EXORBITANT

EXPEL

EXPELLED

EXPERIENTIAL

EXTOL OR EXTOLL

EXTOLLED

EXTRACURRICULAR

EXTRAVAGANT

EYE-OPENER

EYETEETH

F

FABRICATE

FACADE

FACILE

FACSIMILE

FACTOR

FAHRENHEIT

FAINT (pass out; see "feint")

FAIR (attractive; just; carnival; see "fare")

FAIT ACCOMPLI

FALLACY

FALLIBLE

FALSIFY

FARE (price charged to transport; to get along; see "fair")

FARTHER (more distant; see "further")

FARTHEST

FASCINATE

FASHIONABLE

FAVORABLE

FAZE (to disturb composure; see "phase")

FEIGN

FEINT (trick; see "faint")

FEMININE

FEROCIOUS

FESTIVAL

FIANCÉ (betrothed man; see "fiancée")

FIANCÉE (betrothed woman; see "fiancé")

FIERCE

FIERY

FILIPINO

FINESSE

FIRSTHAND

FIRST-RATE

FLABBERGAST

FLACCID

FLAKY OR FLAKEY

FLAMBOYANT

FLAMMABLE

FLEDGLING

FLEXIBLE

FLIMSY

FLIPPANT

FLOPPY DISK

FLORESCENT (flowering; see "fluorescent")

FLOURISH

FLUCTUATE

FLUENT

FLUORESCENT (type of lighting; see "florescent")

FLUORIDE

FLY-BY-NIGHT

FOCUS

FOLIAGE

FONT

FOOLHARDY

FORBEAR (to leave alone; see "forebear")

FORCIBLE

FOREBEAR (ancestor; see "forbear")

FOREBODE

FORECAST

FORECLOSE

FOREFRONT

FOREIGN

FOREKNOWLEDGE

FORENSIC

FORESEE

FORESIGHT

FOREWORD (beginning comments for a book, usually written by one other than the author; see "forward")

FORMIDABLE

FORSAKE

FORSYTHIA

FORT (fortified place; see "forte")

FORTE (strong point; loud musical passage; see "fort")

FORTITUDE

FORWARD (at the beginning; see "foreword")

FOUL (offensive to the senses; out of bounds; see "fowl")

FOWL (bird; see "foul")

FRANCHISE

FRAUDULENT

FRIVOLOUS

FRONTISPIECE

FULFILL

FULFILLMENT

FULLNESS

FURNITURE

FURTHER (extending beyond; to move forward; see "farther")

FURTHEST

FUTILE

G

GALVANIZE

GASEOUS

GASOLINE

GAUCHE (lacking social grace)

GAUNTLET OR GANTLET

GENEALOGY

GENERIC

GENEROUS

GENETICS

GENUINE

GERMANY

GESTATE

GHASTLY

GHETTO

GIBE (to tease; see "jibe")

GIGANTIC

GLAMOUR OR GLAMOR

GLIMPSE

GLOSSARY

GNARL

GNAW

GORGEOUS

GORILLA (large ape; see "guerrilla")

GRADUATE

GRAMMAR

GRANDEUR

GRAVITATE

GRECIAN

GREECE

GRIEVOUS

GRIP (to hold firmly; see "gripe" and "grippe")

GRIPE (grievance; to complain; see "grip" and "grippe")

GRIPPE (influenza; see "grip" and "gripe")

GROTESQUE

GRUDGE

GUARANTEE (to pledge security; see "guaranty")

GUARANTY (something given as security; see "guarantee")

GUERRILLA OR GUERILLA (soldier; see "gorilla")

GUIDANCE

GULLIBLE

GUTTURAL

GYMNASIUM

H

HABEAS CORPUS

HABITANT

HAGGLE

HAIL (precipitation as ice; to call; see "hale")

HAIR (filaments; see "hare" and "heir")

HALE (healthy; see "hail")

HALLUCINATE

HANDICAP

HANDKERCHIEF

HANDYMAN

HANGAR (airplane shelter; see "hanger")

HANGER (that which hangs; see "hangar")

HARANGUE

HARASS

HARBOR

HARE (rabbit; see "hair" and "heir")

HASSLE

HEADACHE

HEEBIE-JEEBIES

HEGEMONY

HEINOUS

HEIR (one who inherits; see "hair" and "hare")

HEMISPHERE

HEMORRHAGE

HEMORRHOID

HERESY

HERITAGE

HEROES (great, brave people)

HEROS (sandwiches)

HESITATE

HEYDAY

HIATUS

HIERARCHY

HILARIOUS

HISTRIONIC

HOARD (see "horde")

HOCUS-POCUS

HOI POLLOI

HOLIDAY

HOLOCAUST

HOMAGE

HOMICIDE

HOODWINK

HORDE (large group; see "hoard")

HOSIERY

HOSPITABLE

HOSTILE (angry)

HULLABALOO

HUMAN

HUMANE

HUMDRUM

HUMERUS (bone of upper arm; see "humorous")

HUMOROUS (funny; see "humerus")

HURRICANE

HYDRAULIC

HYGIENE

HYMN (religious song)

HYPERBOLE (exaggeration)

HYPOCRISY

HYPOTHESIS

HYPOTHETICAL

HYSTERIA

I

ICICLE

IDENTICAL

IDEOLOGY

IDIOSYNCRASY

IDLE (inactive; see "idol" and "idyll")

IDOL (object of adoration; see "idle" and "idyll")

IDYLL OR IDYL (literary form; see "idle" and "idol"

IGNITE

ILLEGIBLE

ILLEGITIMATE

ILLICIT (unlawful; see "elicit")

ILLINOIS

ILLUMINATE

ILLUSION (unreal perception; see "allusion")

IMBECILE

IMBROGLIO

IMMACULATE

IMMANENT (inherent; see "eminent" and "imminent")

IMMIGRATE (to move into; see "emigrate")

IMMINENT (impending; see "eminent" and "immanent")

IMMOVABLE

IMPARTIAL

IMPASSABLE (not passable; see "impassible")

IMPASSE

IMPASSIBLE (incapable of suffering or feeling; see "impassable")

IMPECCABLE

IMPEDE

IMPLACABLE

IMPLEMENT

IMPLICATE

IMPLICIT

IMPROMPTU

IMPUGN

IMPUNITY

INACCESSIBLE

INACCURATE

INADEQUATE

INADMISSIBLE

INADVERTENT

INADVISABLE

INAUDIBLE

INCAPACITATE

INCENDIARY

INCESSANT

INCHOATE

INCIDENT

INCITE (to stir up; compare "insight")

INCOMMUNICABLE

INCOMMUNICADO

INCOMPARABLE

INCOMPATIBLE

INCOMPETENT

INCONCEIVABLE

INCONSISTENT

INCORRIGIBLE

INCREDIBLE

INCREDULOUS

INDECENT

INDECIPHERABLE

INDECISIVE

INDEFENSIBLE

INDEFINITE

INDEMNIFY

INDEMNITY

INDEPENDENT

INDISCERNIBLE

INDISCREET (imprudent; see "indiscrete")

INDISCRETE (not separated; see "indiscreet")

INDISPENSABLE

INDOCTRINATE

INEDIBLE

INEFFECTIVE

INEFFECTUAL

INEFFICIENT

INELIGIBLE

INEPT (clumsy)

INEQUITY (injustice)

INEVITABLE

INFALLIBLE

INFLEXIBLE

INGENIOUS (clever; see "ingenuous")

INGENUOUS (naive; see "ingenious")

INGREDIENT

INHERENT

INIMICAL

INITIATE

INNOCUOUS

INNUENDO

INOCULATE

INSATIABLE

INSIGHT (see "incite")

INSTALL

INSTANTANEOUS

INSTILL

INSURANCE

INTEGRATE

INTELLIGIBLE

INTERCEDE

INTERFERE

INTERROGATE

INTESTATE

INTIMATE

INTRIGUE

INVEIGH

INVINCIBLE

IRAQ

IRASCIBLE

IRIDESCENCE
IRRECONCILABLE
IRREPARABLE
IRRESISTIBLE
IRRETRIEVABLE
IRREVERSIBLE
IRREVOCABLE
IRRITATE
ISAIAH
ISLAND
ISRAEL
ISTHMUS
ITINERANT
ITS (possessive)
IT'S (contraction of "it is")

J

JAGUAR
JANITOR
JAUNDICE
JEALOUS
JEJUNE
JEWELRY
JIBE (to shift suddenly, as
   in sailing; to agree; see
   "gibe")
JODHPUR
JOIE DE VIVRE
JOURNALISM
JUDGMENT OR JUDGEMENT

K

KAFFEEKLATSCH
KAMIKAZE
KARATE
KEOGH
KHAKI
KICKBACK
KILOBYTE
KILOGRAM
KILOMETER
KINDERGARTEN
KNAPSACK
KNEAD (to press)
KNICKKNACK
KNOW-HOW
KNOWLEDGE
KNOWLEDGEABLE
KOWTOW
KUDOS

L

LABEL
LABORATORY
LABYRINTH
LACERATE
LACKADAISICAL
LAISSEZ-FAIRE
LAMINATE
LANDSCAPE
LANGUOROUS

LARYNGITIS

LASCIVIOUS

LAUDABLE

LAUGHABLE

LAVATORY

LEAD (to guide; the heavy metal; see "led")

LED (past tense of "lead"; see "lead")

LEDGER

LEGIBLE

LEGITIMATE

LENIENT

LESSEE

LESSER (smaller; inferior; see "lessor")

LESSOR (one who leases; see "lesser")

LETTUCE

LEVERAGE

LIABLE (responsible; see "libel")

LIBEL (written defamation; see "liable")

LIEUTENANT

LIGHTENING (getting lighter; see "lightning")

LIGHTNING (electrical flash; see "lightening")

LIMOUSINE

LINEAR

LINGERIE

LINGUIST

LIQUEUR (sweetened liquor; see "liquor")

LIQUOR (alcoholic drink; see "liqueur")

LITERACY

LITIGATE

LOATH (hesitant; see "loathe")

LOATHE (to hate; see "loath")

LOITER

LOOSE (slack; see "lose")

LOQUACIOUS

LOSE (to part with; see "loose")

LOUISIANA

LOUNGE

LOVABLE

LOZENGE

LUBRICATE

LUMINARY

LUNCHEON

M

MACABRE

MACHINATION

MACROPROGRAMMING

MADEMOISELLE

MAGNA CUM LAUDE

MAGNANIMOUS

MAGNATE (powerful person; see "magnet")

MAGNET (magnetic or charged object; see "magnate")

MAÎTRE D'HOTEL

MALAISE

MALIGN

MALLEABLE

MANEUVER

MANIKIN OR MANNIKIN (dwarf; see "mannequin")

MANILA

MANNEQUIN (tailor's dummy; see "manikin")

MANSION

MANUFACTURE

MANUSCRIPT

MARIJUANA OR MARIHUANA

MARKDOWN (a lowered price)

MARK DOWN (to lower a price)

MARKUP (a raised price)

MARK UP (to raise a price)

MARRIAGE

MARSHAL OR MARSHALL (officer; see "martial")

MARSHAL OR MARSHALL (to place in proper positions)

MARTIAL (military; see "marshal")

MASCULINE

MASSACHUSETTS

MATERIAL (substance; see "materiel")

MATERIEL (equipment; see "material")

MATHEMATICS

MAUSOLEUM

MAXIMIZE

MAYONNAISE

MEAGER OR MEAGRE

MEDAL (award; see "meddle," "metal," and "mettle")

MEDDLE (interfere; see "medal," "metal," and "mettle")

MEDICINE

MEDIEVAL

MEDIOCRE

MEDITERRANEAN

MEGABYTE

MÉLANGE OR MELANGE

MEMENTO

MEMORABILIA

MEMORABLE

MEMORANDUM

MENAGERIE

MENOPAUSE

MENSTRUATE

MERCENARY

MESSIAH

METAL (the inorganic substance; see "medal," "meddle," and "mettle")

METAMORPHOSIS

METAPHOR

METICULOUS

METTLE (vigor or spiritual strength; see "medal," "meddle," and metal")

MEZZANINE

MICHIGAN

MICROCOMPUTER

MICROSCOPE

MIDGET

MILLENNIUM

MILLIGRAM

MILLIMETER

MILLION

MIMEOGRAPH

MINER (one who mines; see "minor")

MINESTRONE

MINIATURE

MINIMIZE

MINNESOTA

MINOR (younger or lesser; see "miner")

MISANTHROPE

MISCONSTRUE

MISSAL (prayer book; see "missile")

MISSILE (weapon; see "missal")

MISSISSIPPI

MISSIVE

MISSPELL

MISSTATE

MITIGATE

MNEMONIC (assisting memory)

MNEMONICS (memory technique)

MOBILE

MODERATE

MOLECULE

MONARCH

MONASTERY

MONITOR

MONOPOLY

MONUMENT

MORAL

MORALE

MORASS

MORIBUND

MORN (morning; see "mourn")

MORTAL

MOURN (to grieve; see "morn")

MOUSTACHE OR MUSTACHE

MOVABLE

MUCOUS (adjective meaning slimy; see "mucus")

MUCUS (noun meaning secretion; see "mucous")

MULTIMILLIONAIRE

MULTINATIONAL

MUNICIPAL

MURMUR

MUSCLE (body tissue; see "mussel")

MUSEUM

MUSLIM

MUSSEL (type of shellfish; see "muscle")

MYSTERY

MYSTIC

MYSTIQUE

N

NAÏVE OR NAIVE

NAÏVETÉ

NASAL

NAUSEA

NAVAL (of the navy; see "navel")

NAVEL (belly button; orange; see "naval")

NECESSARY

NECESSITATE

NEMESIS

NICOTINE

NINETEEN

NINETIETH

NINETY

NOMENCLATURE

NOMINATE

NONPAREIL

NON SEQUITUR

NOTABLE

NOTICEABLE

NOUVEAU RICHE

NUTRITION

O

OBEDIENT

OBESE

OBNOXIOUS

OBSTINATE

OCCASION

OCCUPATIONAL

OCCUPY

OCCURRENCE

ODYSSEY

OFFENSE

OFTEN

OMELET

OMISSION

OMIT

ONEROUS

ONUS

OPAQUE

OPHTHALMOLOGY

OPPOSITE (completely different)

ORPHAN

OSCILLATE

OSSIFY

OSTRACIZE

OXYGEN

P

PACIFY

PAGEANT

PALATE (roof of the mouth; see "palette" and "pallet")

PALETTE (painter's board; see "palate" and "pallet")

PALLET (thin mattress; see "palate" and "palette")

PANTOMIME

PAPIER-MÂCHÉ

PARACHUTE

PARALLEL

PARALYSIS

PARALYZE

PARASITE

PARE (to trim)

PARI-MUTUEL

PARLIAMENT

PAROCHIAL

PART-TIME

PASSABLE

PASTIME

PATINA

PATRIOT

PAUCITY

PECCADILLO

PEER (equal; to look; see "pier")

PENANCE

PENDANT (ornament; see "pendent")

PENDENT (hanging; see "pendant")

PENETRATE

PENICILLIN

PENINSULA

PENULTIMATE

PER ANNUM

PER CAPITA

PERCEIVE

PER DIEM

PERENNIAL

PERMANENCE

PERQUISITE (privilege; see "prerequisite")

PETITE (small)

PHARMACY

PHASE (period of time; see "faze")

PHENOMENON, PL. PHENOMENA

PHILANTHROPY

PHILIPPINES

PHYSIQUE

PIÈCE DE RÉSISTANCE

PIER (ship dock; see "peer")

PIGEON (bird)

PILLAR

PIMENTO, PL. PIMENTOS

PIQUE (anger)

PLACATE

PLAIN (undecorated; flat land; see "plane")

PLANE (airplane; flat surface; see "plain")

PLATEAU

PLAUSIBLE

PLAYWRIGHT

PLEDGE

PNEUMATICS

PNEUMONIA

POGROM

POIGNANT

POLARIZE

POPULACE (a region's inhabitants; see "populous")

POPULOUS (densely inhabited; see "populace")

POSSESS

POSTDOCTORAL

PRECEDE (to come before; see "proceed")

PRECEDENT (that which comes before; see "president")

PREEMINENT

PREEMPT

PREMIER (first in rank; see "premiere")

PREMIERE (first performance; see "premier")

PREPOSSESS

PREREQUISITE (necessary condition; see "perquisite")

PREROGATIVE

PRESCRIBE (to dictate; see "proscribe")

PRESENCE

PRESENTIMENT (premonition; see "presentment")

PRESENTMENT (act of presenting; see "presentiment")

PRESIDENT (chief; see "precedent")

PRINCIPAL (head of a school; sum of money; most important; see "principle")

PRINCIPLE (guiding law; see "principal")

PROCEED (to continue; see "precede")

PROCESSION (parade)

PROCRASTINATE

PROLOGUE

PROMINENT

PRONOUNCE

PRONOUNCEMENT

PRONUNCIATION

PROPHECY (prediction; see "prophesy")

PROPHESY (to predict; see "prophecy")

PROPHET (one who predicts)

PROPITIOUS

PROSCRIBE (to forbid; see "prescribe")

PRO TEM

PROVABLE

PROXY

PSEUDONYM

PSYCHIATRY

PSYCHOANALYSIS

PSYCHOLOGY

PSYCHOTHERAPY

PUGNACIOUS

PUNCTILIOUS

PUNCTUAL

PUNCTUATE

PYRRHIC

Q

QUASI

QUAY (wharf)

QUEASY

QUEUE (line of people)

QUID PRO QUO

R

RACISM

RACONTEUR

RADIANT

RAIMENT

RAISON D'ÊTRE

RANCOR

RARELY

RARITY

RASPBERRY

RATABLE

RATIONALE

RAUCOUS

RAVENOUS

RAVIOLI

RAZE (tear down)

REALTOR (collective mark)

REALTY

RECALCITRANT

RECAPITULATE

RECEDE

RECEIVE

RECOMMEND

RECOMMIT

RECOMPENSE

RECONCILE

RECONNAISSANCE

RECONNOITER

RECREATE (to refresh; see "re-create")

RE-CREATE (to create again; see "recreate")

RECREATION

REGALE (to entertain)

REIGN (to rule; see "rein")

REIN (strap; see "reign")

REINSURE

RELEVANT

RENAISSANCE

RENDEZVOUS

RENOUNCE

RENUNCIATION

REPEAT

REPETITION

REPEL

REPELLENT

REPENT

REPENTANCE

REPERTOIRE

REPERTORY

REPLACE

REPLACEMENT

REQUISITE

RESCUE

RESISTER (one who resists; see "resistor")

RESISTOR (electrical device; see "resister")

RESORT (vacation spa; see "re-sort")

RE-SORT (to sort again; see "resort")

RESPONSIBLE

RESTAURANT

RESTAURATEUR

RESUME (to begin again; see "résumé")

RÉSUMÉ, RESUME, OR RESUMÉ (summary; see "resume")

RESUSCITATE

RETICENT

REVENUE

REVERENCE

REVERENT

RHAPSODY

RHETORIC

RHYME (similar poetic sounds)

RHYTHM

RICOCHET

RIGHT (correct; see "rite")

RISKINESS

RITE (ceremony; see "right")

ROGUE

ROOKIE

ROSE (flower; see "rosé")

ROSÉ (wine; see "rose")

ROUT (defeat; see "route")

ROUTE (highway; see "rout")

RUDIMENT

RUDIMENTARY

RUIN (to destroy)

S

SABOTAGE

SABOTEUR

SACCHARIN (sweet compound; see "saccharine")

SACCHARINE (sweet; ingratiating; see "saccharin")

SACRAMENT

SACRIFICE

SALABLE

SALMON

SALMONELLA

SALON (elegant living room; see "saloon")

SALOON (barroom or ship's cabin; see "salon")

SANDWICH

SAN FRANCISCO

SANGFROID

SANGUINE

SANITARIUM *OR* SANATORIUM

SAPPHIRE

SARCASM

SATELLITE

SAUCER

SAUERBRATEN

SAUERKRAUT

SAVIOR

SAVOIR FAIRE

SAXOPHONE

SCALPEL

SCARCITY

SCHISM

SCIATICA

SCINTILLATE

SCION

SCISSORS

SCOUNDREL

SCRIP (temporary paper currency; see "script")

SCRIPT (text of a drama; see "scrip")

SCRUPLE

SCULL (racing boat; see "skull")

SCURRILOUS

SCUTTLEBUTT

SEAR (to burn; see "seer" and "sere")

SECEDE

SECRET

SECRETE

SEDENTARY

SEER (predictor of future; see "sear" and "sere")

SEGREGATE

SEIZE

SEMIANNUAL

SEMICOLON

SENATE

SENSIBLE

SENTENTIOUS

SEPARATE

SERE (withered; see "sear" and "seer")

SERF (peasant; see "surf")

SERGEANT

SERIOUS

SEW (to stitch; see "sow")

SEWAGE

SEWER (one who sews; channel for waste)

SEWERAGE

SHEAR (to cut; see "sheer")

SHEER (transparent; going straight up; see "shear")

SHENANIGAN

SHEPHERD

SHERBET *OR* SHERBERT

SHERIFF

SIEGE

SIGHT (faculty of seeing; see "cite" and "site")

SILHOUETTE

SITE (place; see "cite" and "sight")

SKILLFUL

SKULDUGGERY

SKULL (bones of the head; see "scull")

SLEAZY

SLEIGH (large sled)

SMORGASBORD

SNAFU

SOBRIETY

SOBRIQUET

SOCIABLE

SOLACE

SOLDER

SOLDIER

SOLITUDE

SOLVABLE

SOMERSAULT

SOOTH (truth; see "soothe")

SOOTHE (to comfort; see "sooth")

SOPHISTICATE

SOPHOMORE

SOUVENIR

SOVEREIGN

SOW (to plant seeds; see "sew")

SOWER (one who plants; see "sewer")

SPAGHETTI

SPECIES (kind)

SPECIMEN

SPECTACLE

SPECTER

SPECULATE

SPONGE

SQUEAMISH

SQUIRREL

STAMINA

STAMPEDE

STANCH (to stop the flow; see "staunch")

STANZA

STATIONARY (not moving; see "stationery")

STATIONERY (writing supplies; see "stationary")

STATUE

STATURE

STATUTE

STAUNCH (strong or solid; see "stanch")

STEALTH

STENCIL

STEREOTYPE

STERILE

STRAIGHT (without curves; see "strait")

STRAIT (narrow passage; see "straight")

STRATEGY

STRENUOUS

STREPTOCOCCUS

STYROFOAM

SUAVE

SUBLIMATE

SUBORDINATE

SUBPOENA

SUBSEQUENT

SUBTERRANEAN

SUBTLE

SUBTLETY

SUBTLY

SUCCESSFUL

SUCCESSION

SUE

SUICIDE

SUIT (clothes; to fit; see "suite")

SUITE (group of rooms; see "suit")

SUMMARY (short restatement; see "summery")

SUMMERY (like summer; see "summary")

SUNBATH

SUNBATHE

SUNDAE (ice-cream dessert; see "Sunday")

SUNDAY (day of week; see "sundae")

SUPERCILIOUS

SUPERSEDE

SUPERSTITION

SUPPLEMENT

SUPREMACY

SURF (waves; see "serf")

SURRENDER

SURREPTITIOUS

SURROGATE

SURVEILLANCE

SUSCEPTIBLE

SUSPENSE

SYNONYM

SYNONYMOUS

SYNTHESIZE

SYSTOLIC

T

TACIT

TACITURN

TANGIBLE

TAUGHT (past tense of "teach"; see "taut")

TAUT (tight; see "taught")

TAXABLE

TAX-EXEMPT

TECHNICIAN

TECHNIQUE

TEENAGE

TEETOTALER OR TEETOTALLER

TEMPERATURE

TENUOUS

TENURE

TEPEE

TERRA FIRMA

TERRARIUM

TERRITORY

TÊTE-À-TÊTE, PL. TÊTE-À-TÊTES OR TÊTES-À-TÊTE

THEIR (belonging to them; see "there" and "they're")

THERE (that place; see "their" and "they're")

THERMOMETER

THESAURUS

THEY'RE (contraction of "they are"; see "their" and "there")

THOROUGH

THOUSAND

THRESHOLD

THROUGH (finished; by way of)

THUNDEROUS

THWART

TOBACCO

TOCSIN (alarm bell; see "toxin")

TOILET (bathroom fixture; see "toilette")

TOILETTE (fashionable attire; see "toilet")

TOLERANT

TOMORROW

TONSIL

TORT (wrongful civil act; see "torte")

TORTE (kind of cake; see "tort")

TORTUOUS (winding; see "torturous")

TORTUROUS (relating to torture; painful; see "tortuous")

TOUPEE

TOUR DE FORCE

TOXIC

TOXIN (poison; see "tocsin")

TRACEABLE

TRACT (pamphlet)

TRAITOR

TRAITOROUS

TRANSCEND

TRANSIENT

TRAPEZE

TRAUMA

TRAVELER

TRAVELING

TREASURE

TREATISE

TRIGLYCERIDE

TROOP (group of soldiers;
   see "troupe")

TROPHY

TROUPE (group of
   performers; see
   "troop")

T-SHIRT

TURQUOISE

TWELFTH

TWELVE

TYPECAST (to put in a role
   conforming with
   personal traits)

TYRANNY

U

UBIQUITOUS

UKULELE

ULTIMATUM

UMBRELLA

UNACCUSTOMED

UNALTERABLE

UNANIMITY

UNCOMMITTED

UNCOMMUNICATIVE

UNDERRATE

UNFORGETTABLE

UNINTELLIGIBLE

UNIQUE

UNNECESSARY

UNOCCUPIED

UNPARALLELED

UNPRECEDENTED

UNPREDICTABLE

UNPRINCIPLED

UNSUCCESSFUL

UNWIELDY

UPROARIOUS

URBAN (referring to a city;
   see "urbane")

URBANE (polished; see
   "urban")

V

VACATION

VACCINATE

VACILLATE

VACUUM

VAGUE

VAIN (conceited; useless; see "vane" and "vein")

VALEDICTORY

VANE (indicates wind direction; see "vain" and "vein")

VARIABLE

VARIOUS

VEGETABLE

VEIL (covering)

VEIN (blood vessel; see "vain" and "vane")

VELOCITY

VENGEANCE

VERBATIM

VERBIAGE

VERISIMILITUDE

VERTICAL

VETERINARY

VICHYSSOISE

VICISSITUDE

VIGNETTE

VIGOROUS

VINAIGRETTE

VINDICTIVE

VIOLATE

VIOLENT

VIRILE

VIS-À-VIS

VISIBLE

VITAMIN

VOCIFEROUS

VOLUBLE

VORACIOUS (ravenous)

VOYEUR

W

WAIST (human midsection; see "waste")

WAIVE (to forgo; see "wave")

WAIVER (act of abandoning a right; see "waver")

WALLPAPER

WARE (manufactured item; see "where")

WARFARE

WARRIOR

WASHABLE

WASTE (to use inefficiently; see "waist")

WAVE (to flutter; see "waive")

WAVER (to vacillate; see "waiver")

WEAK (not strong; see "week")

WEAK-KNEED

WEALTH

WEAN (to withdraw from breast-feeding; see "ween")

WEAPON

WEATHER (climate; see "whether")

WEEK (seven days; see "weak")

WEEN (to suppose; see "wean")

WEIGH (to measure heaviness)

WELFARE

WET (watery; see "whet")

WHALE (large sea mammal)

WHERE (in what place; see "ware")

WHEREVER

WHET (to sharpen; see "wet")

WHETHER (if; see "weather")

WHOLE (complete)

WIELD

WILLFUL

WILLPOWER

WITCH (worker of magic)

WITTINGLY

WONDROUS

WORKABLE

WORRISOME

WRAITH

WREATH (garland; see "wreathe")

WREATHE (to interweave; see "wreath")

WRECK (to destroy)

WRESTLE

WRETCH (miserable person)

Y

YACHT

YOGURT *OR* YOGHURT

YOUR (possessive of "you"; see "you're")

YOU'RE (contraction of "you are"; see "your")

Z

ZEAL

ZEALOT

ZOOLOGY

ZUCCHINI